GOD *you're* BREAKING *my* HEART

What is God's Response to Suffering & Evil?

BRIAN GROGAN SJ

MESSENGER
PUBLICATIONS
JESUITS *in* IRELAND

First published 2016 by Messenger Publications

ISBN 978-1-910248-15-7

Designed by Messenger Publications Design Department
Typeset in Baskerville & Avenir
Printed in Ireland by Colour World Print Ltd

MESSENGER
PUBLICATIONS
JESUITS in IRELAND

Messenger Publications,
37 Lower Leeson Street, Dublin 2
www.messenger.ie

'O, that my monk's robe
were wide enough
to gather up the suffering people of this floating world'
- Ryokan

CONTENTS

ACKNOWLEDGEMENTS

This book has been a long time in the making. My sincere thanks to my teachers of many years ago who pointed out to me a credible and reliable approach to the subject of suffering and evil. Thanks to all my companions on the journey who have shared their personal stories and challenged me to match theory with raw and painful experience. I mention especially my friends in the Ignatian Group over the past twenty-five years, and more recently the participants in the Sion Hill Class of Autumn 2015, who helped me to articulate the dynamic of this book a bit better.

In particular I wish to thank my brethren who reside in the Jesuit Nursing Home in Dublin and whom I join for the celebration of the Eucharist on Sundays. Their silent acceptance of their varying situations is an ongoing lesson for me. I shall mention them again later.

My sincere gratitude to Patrick Gallagher for his wise theological comments; to Phyllis Brady who read through the final drafts and suggested amendments; to Anne Lyons, Maeve McEvoy, and others whose support kept me going at difficult stages; also to Cecilia West and Sarah Brady of Messenger Publications, who kept me at my task, and to Paula Nolan for her sensitive cover and overall design. Finally, my thanks to Fiona Halpin who responded to my secretarial requests with gracious efficiency.

Some of the raw material for this book has been used elsewhere in my writings, but is treated here from a new point of view. Human stories are multi-faceted!

Jesuit House of Writers
35 Lower Leeson St
Dublin 2

INTRODUCTION

To write a satisfactory book on suffering and evil is beyond my capacity. I have struggled in writing these pages, and you will struggle in reading them. Evil is a dark mystery. Each of us has our own story in which suffering and evil are personalised; each of us endures in their own way. On each topic raised, some readers may want more and others less. As C S Lewis observes, God tells no one any story but their own, and my thoughts can at best only offer hints as to where needed light may be found.

Not only is it demanding to try to get some understanding of suffering and evil, but each of us also contributes to the underlying problem. The line dividing good and evil cuts through the heart of every human being, as Solzhenitsyn says in his *The Gulag Archipelago*. It is easy to denounce evildoers, but more difficult to understand them. But that means that we, who are at best imperfect, have a hard time understanding ourselves as well as others.

Only when the history of this world is drawn to a close will the quasi-infinity of interactions that bring suffering and evil yield up their meaning. The full interpretation will come not from human effort but from divine illumination. Only then will we be able to say, 'Was it not necessary that we should suffer these things and so enter into glory?'

What does this book offer? Shakespeare offers a hint in *Henry V*: *'There is some soul of goodness in things evil, would men observingly distil it out'*. This 'soul of goodness' is our quest. In Christian understanding it is provided by God visibly active in Christ the Son of God, who is the light that shines in the darkness and which the darkness cannot overcome.

This book offers hope and challenge. We use up a vast amount of energy talking about evil; we try to understand how people can do the dreadful things they do; we stand away from them; we fear to get involved; we try to avoid a numbing despair or cynicism. But we need to liberate this energy, and by appropriating the divine response to evil, put our energy to work for a better world. Bishop Desmond Tutu sets the agenda: '*We are made for goodness. We are made for love. We are made for friendliness. We are made for togetherness. We are made for all of the beautiful things that you and I know. We are made to tell the world that there are no outsiders. All are welcome: black, white, red, yellow, rich, poor, educated, not educated, male, female, gay, straight, all, all, all. We all belong to this family, this human family, God's family.*'

Why the title? Firstly it was chosen because I have heard it as the spontaneous cry of many an anguished heart. But it also hints at what is going on deeper down. The American writer Saul Bellow observes somewhere that suffering can break open the human heart, and that there is a rumour that love may also do so. My title, then, has a double meaning: the slow sad music of humankind can indeed break our hearts; but God allows and uses suffering only to enlarge our heart's capacity for that greater love that is its destiny.

As for the 'gleams of light', Hopkins speaks of moments when the light shines through our gloom: '*Across my foundering deck shone a beam, an eternal beam*'. The glimmers of light offered by the Christian tradition can become a steady beam which can enable us to find our way home, even in heavy seas.

Grappling with evil is not just an intellectual amusement: it transforms human living. If we do not transform our pain, we will most assuredly transmit it, as Richard Rohr says. Faced with evil we can become bitter and blaming, negative and closed; or we can become positive and trusting, resilient and patient, and more deeply engaged in the divine struggle to bring good out of evil. Not to overcome the darkness is to be overcome by it.

PART ONE: EXPLORING THE PROBLEM OF EVIL

STARTING POINTS

Jigsaws and Apple Tarts

An image that helps me with the mystery of suffering and evil is the humble jigsaw puzzle. When I was young and the day was wet, I loved to pour out the bits of a puzzle on a large enamel tray. Slowly I would construct the outer frame of the picture, and when that was done, I'd get going on the inside parts. Mostly I'd finish the puzzle eventually, sometimes with a little adult help.

But not always. Not if the cover picture was fuzzy rather than clearly defined, nor if bits were missing or had got mixed up with other puzzles. And of course, if someone upset the tray – my elder brother or the cat were prime suspects! – I'd have to start all over again.

The jigsaw with its dependable outer frame can provide us with an image to help us see that there are *limits* to suffering and evil. *'And light shines in the darkness, and darkness could not overpower it'* (John 1:5). Not that we get *straight* lines, because evil is unpredictable and disorderly, but we are given an awareness of the boundaries which Christian faith provides for our *'mourning and weeping in this valley of tears'*. True, the cover picture of this cosmic jigsaw is fuzzy on detail, and is still being shaped by human history as it moves erratically along. The full picture will not be available for viewing until the history of this world is completed, but it does have a startling and encouraging outline, and sometimes we can see how even the dark elements of our own stories fit in surprisingly well with the outline provided for us.

When my mother rolled pastry for apple tarts, there were always bits which went beyond the edge of the baking plate, but they got tucked in eventually when the chopped apples were added, and they helped increase the crust for which we hungry boys longed. Nothing was wasted. We can rightly hope that, when reworked by God's capable hands, all suffering and evil will be fitted in, with nothing wasted.

Small Bites

These pages offer a set of reflections on suffering and evil. Each chapter is brief and can be read in a short time. But suffering and evil do not yield up their secrets easily. Evil hangs around us like the poison gas that caused such devastation among troops in the trenches of the First World War. It cannot be dealt with directly. I hope simply to help your personal reflection: feel free to disagree with what I say: what matters is that you work out for yourself a better way of understanding the darker side of human life, and that you somehow find God in it.

As with Elephant Pie, take these reflections in small bites! Scattered across the pages are short stories which illustrate an underlying theme – *that God is always working to bring good out of evil.* Occasionally we see good emerging from what is bad, and this pattern gives us hope. If you find some of the theory heavy going, take refuge in these stories, and see if they match in some ways your own experience. My conviction is that God is labouring in your life and mine to make good what is not good: to discover this is to find a treasure.

When I propose that God is labouring to bring good from what is bad, I do not mean that God restores to us the particular good we lost, but that some different good emerges: God does not roll back time and history. Rather like an artist working on a damaged masterpiece, God brings out a new feature which enhances the spoiled original. Think of the challenge faced by a sculptor working on stone rather than bronze. Bronze can be recast whereas with stone the artist has to integrate the damage into a more complex work of art.

Two scriptural examples can help: The *Book of Job* closes with God doubling the fortune of Job, after all his troubles (42:10-17). History is rolled back. This happy resolution of his problems indicates that the episode is an early story. When however the disciples meet the risen Jesus, history is not rolled back. Surprisingly it is the enduring reality of the wounds that guarantees the authenticity of his presence. *'He showed them his hands and his side'* (John 20:20). Later he is named as *'the first-born of the dead'* (Revelation 1:5). *'Our wounds are our glory'* as Julian of Norwich put it in the 14th century. Here history is respected while also being transfigured.

Times of Tranquillity

It is better to reflect on suffering and evil when you are in tranquillity rather than upset. If you postpone your reflection until you are immersed in a tragedy it may well catch you up on all levels and leave you with no heart-space to reflect. Likewise if you are trying to help others who are paralysed with grief, it probably won't help to offer them this book. Better simply to be with them in quiet solidarity, and when and if the time seems right, offer something that may respond to their emerging questions. As I write, reports are coming in that a woman has just lost her husband, two of her children, her mother and her sister in a drowning accident. Silent supportive solidarity is all one can offer in face of such a numbing tragedy.

Getting a perspective on suffering is more a matter of entering into its mystery than of sorting it out. Suffering is a strange land. In a sense, we could say that even God does not understand evil because, as we shall see, there is something about evil that lacks reasonableness. Perhaps God is still puzzled as to why Adam and Eve made such a mess of things when all was so beautifully set up for their enjoyment. On a lighter note, you know the story of Adam and Eve when they were wandering in the desert and saw the Garden of Eden in the distance, with its gates under heavy guard. *'That'* said the oldest child to the others *'is where we used to live before Mum and Dad ate us out of house and home!'*

We will be returning to this issue of the unreasonable factor in evil. But we all know the experience of saying, *'I don't know why I did that!'* We mean that what we did can't be explained fully: something is missing that should be there.

Head and Heart

A contemplative attitude of heart helps as you work along. It is good to ask God to enable you to see what you need to see. You will find that the Holy Spirit will help you. Nuggets of wisdom will come your way, tailor-made for your current situation. You will wonder, happily, where they came from and you will find your own ways of expressing them. Pope Francis lays stress on the wisdom of the faithful, which guides us, the People of God, on our painful pilgrim journey. As we grow older we are meant to be growing in wisdom: we see things in a new way. Not that we crack open the mystery of our lives, but we accommodate ourselves to it. We get a feel for our topic and develop a strange sort of knowledge which earlier thinkers called 'learned ignorance' – by which they meant that the more you know, the more you know you don't know!

One of my relatives works in the UN, which means that every few years the family has to move house. It is always a traumatic event. She has four children and told her family last year that she was having a mid-life crisis and that they must be patient with her. This summer the family got news that they must move again, whereupon her ten-year-old said, *'I think I'm going to have a mid-life crisis!'* Everyone laughed, but from her own troubling experience the mother was able to empathise with the confusion of her son. Often when you have worked through a painful experience which has yielded a positive outcome, you find yourself able to help someone else who is going through something similar. While we must not overstate this, we may see a recurring pattern of good emerging from evil, as in the following account.

THE 'DISAPPEARED'

In the days of the death squads in El Salvador and Argentina, thousands of catechists and others disappeared. In response, the Christians of these countries developed in their liturgy a dramatic way to celebrate their faith, hope and resistance, and to proclaim that their community was strong and would not be extinguished by death. During the liturgy, the list of the 'disappeared' would be read out, and one by one someone would stand and say for the person named: 'Presente!' (Present!). The 'disappeared' indeed were present: each had a unique name and dignity, and each had a voice still, through the mouths of their caring sisters and brothers. The congregation drew strength and courage from them to continue to build the kingdom of God despite the risk of torture and brutal death.

The pattern of good emerging out of evil occurs, but it is not direct, and to look for the wrong thing brings disappointment. In the case above, those who were murdered were gone; they were not miraculously returned to their families or communities. But something new was born: a deep courage that came from above and beyond, enabling the community to continue to witness to God's dream for the world as their dead companions had done.

FOR REFLECTION

What instances can you recall where the response to some evil was surprising, but creative and life-giving?

LIVING WITH MYSTERY

Our lives are wrapped around in mystery. We spend our lives like amateur detectives, asking questions: Why? What? Who? Where? When? How? We are explorers with an insatiable desire for knowledge. Each insight raises further questions, and so it is when we are exploring evil and suffering. They are mysteries, and the best we can do as we proceed is to lay down stepping stones to guide us across a fast-flowing river. To try to explain too much is fatal because we have such limited evidence. Arguing doesn't help: believers and non-believers need to sit on the same side of the table, look out at the same dark realities that beset our common experience, acknowledge that suffering is embedded in human life, listen sincerely to each other, and try to move forward together. Religious belief does not mean that we have all the answers: religion offers only gleams of light, not full illumination.

Throughout this book we will be dealing with the mystery of pain and suffering from a Christian perspective. By the word 'mystery' I mean a reality which is imbued with the hidden presence of God. God is in visible reality but we cannot experience this presence directly and immediately. God is also present at the deeper levels of reality, including our simple prayer, or the sacraments. When Jesus came, he illuminated reality in new ways, disclosing unguessed-at meaning in it, always for our good. As we shall see, he offers essential light on the dark mystery of evil.

Here I name some of the mysteries we will come across in our journey: you may well add more because Christianity is all about one great Mystery: God.

- The mystery of God, who simply IS, and is not to be explained.
- The mystery of the cosmos: why does anything exist, including ourselves?

- ❦ The mystery as to how it can be true that 'when all is said and done, we are infinitely loved'.
- ❦ The mystery of the Incarnation, and why, God likes to come in disguise.
- ❦ The mystery of how the Son of God suffers at human hands and is done away with by evil.
- ❦ The mystery of why God allows free will to bring such evil and suffering into the divine and the human world.
- ❦ The mystery of why God tolerates suffering and the breaking of the human heart.
- ❦ The mystery of human death.
- ❦ The mystery of the Resurrection of Jesus, which gives hope of eternal life to all humankind.
- ❦ The mystery of the slow unfolding of the divine response to suffering and evil.
- ❦ The mystery of how God manages to bring good out of evil.
- ❦ The mystery of how the human epic will end, in glory or tragedy.
- ❦ The mystery of why God judges that human history is worth the cost.

Kindly Light

My humanist friends ask me, *'Why drag in religion when you're talking about evil?'* I answer that I don't believe we can investigate evil adequately without illumination from a higher source. From its beginning, the Hebrew tradition has wrestled with the issue of evil, and the Christian perspective sheds essential light on the problem, without pretending to satisfy all questions. On a dark road even a small torch can help you to read the signposts and struggle along in the right direction. We need God to illuminate our pain and darkness, and so we keep our eye as steadily as we can on the divine light that is offered us. Newman wrote of *'kindly light amid the encircling gloom'*. When kindly light is shared, it enables us to take our next step. This kindly light of God shines in the darkness of human life, and we call it faith, which means that we come to see things the way God sees them. *'Without vision the people perish'* (Proverbs 29:18), and the Christian vision gives us vision and energy to square up to evil and tragedy rather than to crumble before them.

We can be comforted – and comfort others – by the light that the Christian tradition offers. The word *'comfort'* comes from the Latin word for strength or bravery'. So its main meaning is *'to strengthen'* rather than to make us feel good. What is offered by Christian faith helps to guide our footsteps over tough terrain, rather than banish our miseries.

Complaints Against God

I like the title of an older book: *Complaints against God by One of his Creatures*. The author imagines himself squaring up to God after death, and demanding explanations and apology for the existence of suffering and evil in his own life and in the wider world. The fact that the author chooses to remain anonymous allows each of us to add our personal complaints to the list. Only when we meet God face to face will our complaints and queries be fully set at rest.

I also like the 2008 movie *God on Trial*. It is set in a German concentration camp during the Jewish Holocaust of the Second World War. The prisoners put God on trial, and after much argument the prosecutor wins his case: God is responsible for the suffering of the prisoners and has betrayed his people and his covenant. Immediately after the verdict the prison guards burst in and select a number of prisoners for execution. As they are herded off to the gas chamber one asks: *'Now that we have found God guilty, what do we do?'* The prosecutor replies, *'We pray!'* And they do, because God, whether guilty or not, remains their last refuge.

My Personal Credo

Readers have a right to know an author's presuppositions, so here goes for myself as I begin. I believe that the natural world around us hints at the existence of an Originator of extraordinary imagination and power. In other words, I hold that this world is created; that it did not come into being of itself and organise itself into its limitless complexity. I believe that this Originator must be a Person, with mind and will and vision: an impersonal life force could hardly bring a world of persons into existence. I believe further that the inner nature of this Person is revealed to some extent in what is made; that the cosmos is encompassed by beauty and by love, and that we humans are destined to participate in the life of our Originator.

I believe that the One whom we name *'God'* is self-revealing for our sakes, and has shown this most dramatically by entering personally into our world in Jesus Christ; that in the mystery of his Cross and Resurrection evil is radically checked and transformed and eternal life is opened up to us. Further that what we endure in this life can prepare us well for what is to come, by expanding our hearts to a level of love that slowly takes on the contours of God's unrestricted loving of everyone.

I believe however that the Christian life is not just about bearing the pain that comes our way, but rather that it is all about relationships. At the heart of reality are the three divine Persons: they relate together with ecstatic love, and that love flows out to us and to all creation. The cosmos is not an aggregate of bits and bobs linked accidentally, if at all, with one another! Everything is related with everything else, as science affirms. On the human level, God's final intention is a community of love in which all relationships are brought to their full development. The reality of *friendship* catches up the dynamic which God has in mind. Just as the divine Persons are totally FOR one another, they are FOR us too, and we are to be FOR them and one another. We are to catch on to the deepest mystery about us – that we are infinitely loved. Our challenge is to respond by loving God, creation and all our fellow-travellers on this little planet.

Sin, evil and death create a radical challenge to this intended order of things, and only when we meet God directly will we fully grasp how God weaves them into ultimate harmony. I believe that there is no intra-worldly hypothesis that can satisfactorily integrate suffering and evil: that only God can provide the needed framework. The acceptance of the divine resolution of suffering and evil therefore demands faith. But faith is not a leap into the dark so much as a reaching out to *'the true light which enlightens everyone'* (John 1:9).

So much for my efforts to identify my belief. I invite you now to take a moment to identify your personal credo. The word *credo* does not simply mean that I assent to a number of truths about God. It is more personal, and comes from the Latin *(cor do)*, which means *'I give my heart to'*. So the question is, *'To what sort of God can you give your heart?'*

Where's the Problem?

Many people would be willing to believe in God if evil did not exist. But evil does exist as something terrifyingly close. The oppressive reality of evil, however, does not prove the non-existence of God: instead it creates a huge problem for believers, who have to hold in tension both the reality of what is savage and destructive and the existence of a Being who orchestrates the development of the world.

While belief in God *cannot be proved* in scientific fashion, it can be shown that belief in God's existence is *reasonable*. The created world cannot explain itself – it need not exist, yet there it is. As crime writers know so well, the human desire for explanation demands that events that don't have to happen must be explained by something else. Believers find it reasonable to postulate the existence of a self-explanatory and necessary Being who originates all other reality. By 'God' they mean the One who simply IS.

Since neither the existence nor the non-existence of God can be proven scientifically, either stance is a matter of belief. Believers have to work up the arguments for believing in God in the face of evil which most certainly exists. Which is what these pages are about!

A derivative problem for me is that I believe in the possibility that everyone will be saved. But how can this be, given the evil of the world? I discuss the arguments for this hope in *Where To From Here? The Christian Vision of Life After Death*. There I try to show that there is solid ground for belief that God will succeed in gathering everybody into eternal joy. This issue will be discussed in the closing pages of this book.

MATRYONA'S HOUSE

The Russian author, Alexander Solzhenitsyn tells a story which encapsulates something of the mystery of goodness that underpins and transforms the malice and evil of our world.

> *Matryona lives alone in a big dilapidated Siberian house. She is untidy, slovenly, a poor cook, careless of her own meagre possessions, and lives on the edge of destitution. She makes no effort to accumulate things, has no fine clothes. She responds to every call for help, whether by digging potatoes for others or sharing her precious turf with them. Misunderstood and derided, she has lost six children. She keeps a dirty-white goat, a disabled cat, and some*

rubber plants. She refuses to get a pig because pigs are destined for slaughter. The end comes when her family take advantage of her generosity and persuade her to give away most of her wooden house. She helps them to remove what they want, but is killed in the process by a passing train. The author reflects that those who had lived side by side with her had never understood that she was

> *'that righteous person*
> *without whom, as the proverb says,*
> *no village can stand,*
> *nor any city,*
> *nor our whole land'.*

This magnificent tale tells a great truth. It affirms that the human spirit is capable of rising above the pain and toil of life, above the degradation and humiliation imposed by others. When all is stripped away, there can emerge a quality of pure loving of which the possessor may be quite unaware. Human evil can be encompassed and transformed by greatness of heart.

FOR REFLECTION

You may know someone like Matryona: such people are failures by common standards – they seem to be giving their lives away rather than getting them together. Others take advantage of them and abuse their kindness. Do you have something of Matryona's mindset or does she challenge your values and your ways of relating?

OUR EXPERIENCE OF SUFFERING

Experience

It is time to look at our personal experiences of suffering and evil: otherwise we remain on the level of ideas and theory. Throughout our lives we are meant to try to understand our experiences, because it is in them that God is to be found. As the Greeks said, the unexamined life is not worth living. T S Eliot adds that we have many experiences but can miss their meaning. So I will soon invite you to rummage in your storehouse of memories for your experiences of suffering, pain and evil. Then we will look to see how we can make sense of them. Firstly, though, we will clarify the terms we use.

Evil

What do we mean by *evil?* The term is often used to refer to anything that is bad. People speak of the evils of alcohol or power, though neither is bad in itself. Sickness is often referred to as *physical evil*. But for us evil refers to *moral evil*, wrong human actions – what Christian tradition calls *sin*. It denotes whatever is contrary to conscience, morally reprehensible, unjust. Evil occurs when a person deliberately violates the rights of another. Evil is the major cause of human suffering; some say that 95% of the world's pain can be laid at the door of human malice. An example: for marrying the man she loved, Saba's own father shot her in the head, stuffed her in a bag, and dumped her in a river. Then he walked free because of a loophole in his country's laws that allows men to commit so-called 'honour killings.' Here we have evil in brutal form.

For some readers the word 'evil' is menacing: it conjures up a supernatural destructive force, against which they feel powerless. I will say a word later about the notion of a personal force for evil. But the term 'evil' is impossible to avoid – it occurs over 600 times in the Bible.

Suffering

What do we mean by suffering? It is a state of unhappiness, pain, distress, misery, however caused. In its origin the word means that we are *weighed down* by something we are carrying. This is a good description of our everyday experiences of suffering. There are the mundane battle scars, the unhappy experiences arising from our daily interactions with others. On a broader level are violent crime, betrayal, abuse, deceit, oppression, injustice, murder — the raw material for the daily news bulletins. Suffering is a burden which we instinctively try to avoid, because it invades our wellbeing. We all experience it to a greater or lesser extent, and we share in the sufferings of those we know and love, which adds to our personal burden. We mean *'the thousand natural shocks that flesh is heir to'* as Hamlet put it: misfortune, hardship, breakdown, failure, tragedy, death. We think about suffering, try to avoid it, talk about it, cry over it, pray over it, and try to adjust to it: here we will be trying to understand it a little.

The Bible is sometimes referred to as *The Book of Suffering*, and each of us has our own 'secret scripture' of suffering. Suffering is not optional. It is not just 'out there' or in the lives of others. It is written into the fabric of our lives: we may try to dismiss it or ignore it, but it won't go away. *'We are born in others' pain and perish in our own'* as Francis Thompson says. In between birth and death we also endure much pain. The Latin poet Virgil says, *'The world is a world of tears, and the burdens of mortality touch the heart'*. Shakespeare writes, 'Men must *endure* their going hence even as their coming hither' (*King Lear*, Act 5, Scene 2). Jesus says, 'The one who *endures* to the end will be saved' (Mk 13:13). The American author Thoreau remarked long ago that the mass of people *'lead lives of quiet desperation'*. We *endure* much suffering.

The Valley of Darkness

Suffering is ambiguous. It is bad if it breaks our hearts *apart*; but it has some goodness in it if it breaks our hearts *open*. Suffering can harden us and kill us. But it can also shape us for good: we can become more compassionate, gentle, loving, accepting. My title, *God, You're Breaking My Heart*, is open to both interpretations. The aim of the book is to offer you some help *to find your way through* what is bad, and this is hinted at in the best known and most personal of the Psalms, *The Lord Is My Shepherd* (Psalm 23). There the central image is of a good shepherd who, surprisingly, is busy looking after a *single* sheep rather than a large flock. The relationship between shepherd and sheep is intimate. In a few verses, while praising the shepherd, the psalmist refers to himself eighteen times! The shepherd is dependable and intimate, and guides the psalmist through his own dark valleys. Emerging from the darkness, he finds a specially prepared table for two, at which he feasts with God. At funerals such images offer great comfort to the bereaved and gives them hope that the person they loved is now bathed in the eternal loving kindness of God.

My Own Story

My own experience of suffering begins with the dysfunctionality in my family and my family tree. It has taken me many years to acknowledge the flaws and negative traits in my ancestry, but what family is not at least a little dysfunctional? After all, I remind myself, the genealogy of Jesus is sprinkled with murderers, adulterers and harlots; with the proud, the greedy, the bossy, the evildoers. We are in good company with him: all of us share in the inadequacy of the human family and we suffer the effects of the darker aspects of the lives of others, as well as their good qualities. I am part of that dynamic.

To get a grip on the flow of data of my life, I find help in Teilhard de Chardin's division of our lives into the things we accomplish over a lifetime (activities); and the things that befall us over which we have little or no control (passivities). While we may indeed achieve a great

deal in a lifetime, it is in fact the things that *happen* to us which dominate. We have very little control over much of our world – it's a set-up
job! I mean that in the sense that I didn't get to choose my parents or
my family tree, nor to be a healthy baby, nor even to be born at all, for
after my elder brother's birth, my mother had been advised not to risk
having another child. I had no choice between being male or female,
nor was I asked to pick out the unique traits that constitute the bundle
that is me. Nor did I choose where to be born – I made my appear-
ance in Ireland, which remained neutral in the Second World War. If
I had been Jewish and born in mainland Europe, my life would probably ended abruptly in a concentration camp, like the eight-year-old
boy in John Boyne's novel *The Boy in the Striped Pyjamas*.

The Dark Pages

My story continues with the ups and downs of home life, neighbour-
hood, schooling. Over and over I was being shaped by the reality
around me, and both society and Church created a restricting environment. Some of it was good, but there were tears too, rage and frustration, the sense of being treated unfairly. I had a passion for justice
– at least for myself! I tried my best to assert my place in the scheme
of things, but that was a recipe for trouble from others who cut across
my little plans! And so the story unfolded over the years – the disappointments, humiliations, and also the growing awareness that I could
be hurtful to others – a sense of shame that sometimes at least I was
not very nice to know. My perfectionism, adopted early on to protect
me from the dysfunctionality at home, made unfair demands on others, and it is a lifetime's struggle to get free of it.

I was told once, '*You are a just man, but with little love*'. After the shock
and denial, slowly there grew grief at being the cause of others' grief,
at being a disappointment to God and an obstacle to God's project
for the world. I like the present Pope's insistence that he is a sinner,

but *'pitied, redeemed and chosen to serve'*. That's me too! As an aside, I may mention that when the Jesuits gathered in 1974 to study their own identity, they came up with the statement that *'to be a Jesuit is to be a sinner, yet called to be a companion of Jesus as their founder Ignatius was'*. Ignatius, 1491–1556, was a colourful sinner in his earlier years, so I am in good company and need not pass over the *dark* pages of my life! By 'dark' I mean that not only do we endure suffering and pain but we contribute our share. I know what it is like to be the cause of pain to others. My spontaneous approach or stance may jar on others without my intending it, or I may deliberately hurt someone by despising them, putting them down and making them feel bad.

I have not been simply a detached spectator in the drama of life but a participant in the struggle between good and bad, both as victim and as perpetrator. I know what it is like to spoil relationships. I have wasted much time and energy on the wrongdoing of my neighbour while passing over my own failings and my sins of omission. The Eucharist begins with a statement of repentance for what we have done and what we have failed to do. Often I do not know what harm I do, simply by doing nothing. But I find it good to take time to gaze contemplatively on the reality of my life. I invite the Lord to be present, to lead me to see what I need to see: the promise of Jesus to me is that *'the truth will set you free'* (John 8:32) to be a more wholesome presence to others.

Bearing the Pain of Others

The pain of others is a dimension of the suffering in my life. There are books and films I avoid because I cannot bear to think of what others have endured. I find A&E Departments demanding. I thank God that I do not suffer from depression, but I watched it in my mother for eighteen years. No matter how she tried to shake it off, it clung to her like a demon. We both suffered much over those years. Just as we can take joy in the joy of others, we can hurt with others' pain. St Paul says that *'we are one body, and if one part suffers, all suffer together with it'* (1 Corinthians 12:26). I know that to be true. My sister-in-law's death by suicide has affected me deeply, as I shall indicate below. I long to see her again and know that all is now well with her.

I dread interpersonal friction. Resentments, jealousies, fixations, take away my joy – and my sleep – until I deal with them. *'Help me'* a woman said to me recently, *'I had a big row with my sister eleven years ago, and we haven't spoken since. It tortures me. It's like a black cloud.'* I can only guess the pain they have both endured. I watch the news with its daily menu of horror stories, and find it hard to forgive the people of violence. I got help in Brian Lennon's sympathetic book *So You Can't Forgive…* His insights are born out of people's reflection on their experience of the Troubles in Northern Ireland over thirty years. The title alone gives me comfort because unconditional forgiving is so hard. Someone told me that the word 'for-giving' means *'giving to the point of exhaustion'* – and this can be true. It makes great demands on us. Forgiveness has a divine quality about it: we rightly say that to err is human but to forgive is divine.

And so my thread of suffering and evil unfolds through the years. The Church as an institution has brought me deep pain by its insensitivity: women are treated as second-class citizens and are excluded from its decision-making processes; children have endured clerical sexual abuse and the abusers have been shielded from punishment; so much of the laity's God-given talent and creativity have been stifled by over-control, and impossible burdens have been laid on the shoulders of good people through the use of fear and the stifling of conscience. But as a publicly-declared member of the Church, how far have I been complicit in these wrongdoings? Often I dared not speak out; I was compromised and so I added to the problem. As St Augustine and others have said, *'For evil to succeed it is enough for good people to do nothing'.*

Physical suffering is obvious enough: I have had my small share of it. Now the unwelcome visitor we call ageing has come to stay with me, bringing its disturbing diminishments. My seventy-eight years offer plenty of scope for me to explore where suffering, pain and frustration have left their mark; but what I have endured has been tiny, contrasted with the suffering of others around me, and this has made me aware of the kindness of God who has watched over me with delicate care and saved me from much harm. In my later years, I am letting go of what I wanted to be, and settling instead for what I am.

Your Story

So much for me. What spontaneously comes to mind for you at this point? I sketched the story of Matryona, and we each have our own story of suffering and the hard-won wisdom around it. I suggest that you take a page and jot down what comes to mind when you survey the physical, mental, emotional and spiritual dimensions of your life. One experience links to another, because we can't divide our lives into separate compartments. These experiences have helped to make you what you now are. Your story may get longer and longer and seem overwhelming, yet the fact is that *you have coped* – at least in part – with what you have endured, and there lie the glimmers of light that help you to keep going. There is a resilience in you, a capacity to recover from set-backs and to find a new way forward. Through the pain of your life God is constantly drawing you – through thick and thin – to the fullness of life. God is stubbornly committed to you, stays with you through the most awful situations, and finally, even if you are bruised and battered, brings you home.

Recall the story of Saba who was shot, stuffed into a bag and thrown into a river. Amazingly, she survived and is now leading a movement to stop such outrages. God is committed to her, and is glad to have her support now in trying to end a particular evil.

The following incident hints at God's grace winning through in an unexpected way.

HOW TO THANK YOU?

Pedro Arrupe, Superior General of the Jesuits 1965–1983, tells of an experience in a Latin American slum. He had been invited to celebrate Mass in a small open structure, through which cats and dogs came and went as they pleased. The guitarist led the first hymn: 'To love is to give oneself, to forget oneself, by seeking that which can make another happy. How beautiful it is to live for love!' Arrupe was deeply moved as he looked around at the people, their faces hard and tanned by the sun, but lean and drawn by their poverty. Some were in tears. They had nothing, yet were ready to give themselves to make others happy.

Afterwards, one young man said: 'Padre, we are very thankful for our priests: they have taught us to love our enemies. A week ago I had prepared a knife to kill someone whom I hated much, but after I heard the priest explain the Gospel, I went and bought an ice-cream and gave it to my enemy'.

At the end of the celebration a big fearsome-looking man addressed Arrupe: 'Come to my house. I have something to show you'. They climbed a hill in silence until they came to his half-fallen shack: the man made him sit down on a rickety chair. From there the setting sun could be seen. His host said: 'Señor, see how beautiful it is!' They remained silent until the sun disappeared. Then he said: 'I did not know how to thank you for all you have done for us. I have nothing to give you, but I thought you would like to see this sunset. It pleased you, didn't it?' He then guided Arrupe back down the hill to where he was staying.

FOR REFLECTION

This 'big fearsome-looking man' is living in near-destitution, yet he has an appreciation of the beauty of sunsets; he is grateful to Pedro Arrupe for visiting the local slum, and decides to share with him his single treasure. There is a many-layered mystery within this man: sensitivity, gratitude, contemplation. He has risen above the limitations of his circumstances. What is it about him that stands out for you? Does his situation match yours in any way?

CAN WE MAKE SENSE OF EVIL?

Now that we have explored in some small way our *experiences* of suffering and wrongdoing, we can try to make some sense of them. This is our theme, but it is hard work. If my comments are less than fully coherent, it is because I feel like someone doing a painting in the dark. We have trouble enough coping with *physical* misfortunes such as poverty, sickness, death, tsunamis. But when we come to human wrong-doing we are even more out of our depth. At school I was fascinated by mercury. You can see and feel it but it is impossible to hold: it slips away from you. *Moral evil is a bit like handling mercury: it is fascinating but very difficult to grapple with.* We cannot adequately explain it. But going back to the image of the jigsaw, can we find any boundary pieces with which to hem in the unsorted jumble, or must it remain a meaningless pile?

If there were easy answers, we would have had them long ago; but we puzzle all our lives over suffering and wrongdoing. It is a strange land. Questions crowd in on us, and we get no satisfactory answers. We ask, *'What have I done to deserve this?' 'Why should this happen to someone I love who is so good?' 'Is God the cause of tsunamis?' 'A God of love would not allow this.' 'My life is falling apart: where's God?' 'Is there any meaning in all this?'* The problem of suffering and evil tortures the human mind.

'The still, sad music of humanity' – Wordsworth's phrase – continues to play, century after century. Our puzzling will never end in this life. From the time when our remote ancestors first appeared on earth some 300,000 years ago, they must have puzzled over the things that went wrong – injury, violence, famine, death. Early on, they developed belief in local gods – expressing their belief in beings more powerful than themselves, who might be entreated for help in times of need. The Greeks asserted that we humans are made for happiness, so we envy the gods their immortality and incorruptibility; we would

wish to be like them but they are not interested in our misery, and so fate continues to dish out unpalatable menus to us. Such was their interpretation of life: can we offer something better?

Your Philosophy of Evil and Suffering

Each of us develops a personal philosophy of suffering and evil. A 'philosophy' is a framework within which we try to make sense of life's happenings. Your philosophy of life can be different to that of others; it changes as life moves on and ideally will become more comprehensive. These pages are meant to assist that process.

A Jesuit friend of mine died recently in the prime of life – he was sixty. A mourner sympathised with me, saying, '*God took him. It was his time to go…*' This kind of comment leaves me dissatisfied and irritated. How could anyone know another's time to go? And is it true that God has a pre-arranged moment to pluck us from this life? I prefer to think that death comes through natural causes rather than through direct divine intervention.

At another funeral I overheard a mother who had lost her son in tragic circumstances. She said, '*I deserved it. I never thanked God enough for him.*' To which a well-meaning neighbour replied, '*No you don't deserve it: God punishes those he loves. Darkness is the shadow of God's outstretched hand.*' This again irritated me: what sort of God had both of them in mind: a God who would take revenge on someone if they were ungrateful, or punish those he loves? Another neighbour said nothing: he just gave the mother a big hug, something he had never done before for anyone. I found myself silently applauding his gesture of human solidarity. But then it was my turn to respond to the mother's pain.

What would you say or do? Do you know what your philosophy of suffering is? Spend a few moments recalling what comes into your mind when some tragedy touches you.

An Adequate Framework

We need an adequate framework to cope with suffering and evil. If our framework is too narrow, we do violence to some aspect of it. The outer edges of a jigsaw must be long enough to hold all the pieces. Thus in early times people thought eclipses were caused by the gods dragging their chariots across the face of the sun. But this ingenious explanation fell apart when the predictability of eclipses was established. As a small child I was told, *'Thunder is the gods shouting when they're having a row'* – I later learnt that it is produced by the explosive expansion of air heated by a lightning discharge. Likewise, at first glance, some theories about evil are neat and tidy, such as, *'If God existed and were all-powerful and good, there would be no evil in the world. But there is evil. Therefore God does not exist.'* But if in fact God does exist, then that neat framework is too small. Another version of the argument goes, *'If God exists, he must be mad or bad, because no sane or good God would allow evil'*.

But perhaps, just perhaps, – in a large enough framework – suffering and evil can co-exist with a wise and good God? Is it the case that in an expanding universe periodic failures and disasters such as tsunamis and earthquakes are inevitable, and that the slow evolution of humankind from its primitive origins makes us as yet poorly adapted to choose consistently what is good? And is it possible that the waywardness of human free-will can be incorporated into a comprehensive and radical solution to the problem of evil?

Every Little Helps

Our questioning leads to answers which lead to further questions – about life, faith, God, the future of our race. Ours is a pilgrimage that starts at birth – or did it start when all things originated some 13.8 billion years ago? This pilgrimage goes on until we die. But after death does our journey take off in a new way? Are we brought behind the scene of creation into the inner workings of divine energy and creativity? The existence of the cosmos raises the question, 'Who started it?' The wonder of things suggests that the One who creates and sustains everything is totally wonderful. And yet there is the dark side of things, so can we call God 'wonderful' also in relation to that darkness? If God exists, it cannot be as a static Being, a museum piece; instead the Originator must be Pure Energy, Unlimited Imagination, Power, Love Abounding. In death are we perhaps drawn into this divine life, as the Greeks and other early thinkers had hoped? Will this new relationship with the divine bring us immortality and endless joy, and open out into unwearying exploration of the wonders of the galaxies?

Some of those questions can be responded to if you have the time and energy for them. I wrote the book *Where To From Here?* with such issues in mind. But we are small creatures who can have only a dim understanding of what goes on in the divine mind and heart. Yet enough is given us to accept in faith that God knows what he is about, and that God is for our good. The First Vatican Council in 1870 said that we can obtain some understanding of the mysteries of faith, and that this knowledge can be *most fruitful* for us (*fructuosissima* in the Latin!). The same can be said in dealing with suffering and evil. Long ago St Anselm spoke of theology as *faith seeking understanding*, and here we try to make some sense of suffering and evil from the Christian perspective. Buddhism and other religions have their own valuable philosophies of pain and misfortune, but to include them here would make this little book impossibly unwieldy. The Christian vision offers us more than enough to cope with!

The following account illustrates my struggle to come to terms with a family tragedy. A secure framework was suddenly shattered, followed by a slow and painful effort to find another which would do some justice to the new reality.

ALIVE AND HAPPY

My sister-in-law, a wonderful person and gifted in so many ways, took her own life when I was in my early forties. I was in Rome en route to work in Somalia when the news came. I had said a fond goodbye to her a few days earlier.

In her years of depression I had become her confidant and we had grown very close. My family of origin was tiny – my parents and my brother: I had no sisters, so she was my closest female relative apart from my mother. As I flew back from Rome to lead her funeral service, my mind was a whirl of shock, confusion and conflicting emotions. I felt in some way that she had betrayed me by choosing to die immediately after I had left Dublin, and had betrayed my brother and her two boys by setting them adrift to endure the pain of bereavement. I had to cope with the negative attitude of the Catholic Church towards suicide, though the ban on burial in consecrated ground had at least officially eased. While wrestling with such feelings, two lines from the hymn 'The Holy City' popped into my head: 'the gates were open wide, and all who would might enter, and no-one was denied.' These lines sustained me through difficult days, and kept me going during the homily at the funeral Mass.

What good came of it all? Over the long years since then, her death has given me a fellow-feeling for others similarly bereaved, and also a conviction that God can cope with suicide victims and those who mourn them. The God of compassion – compassion means 'to walk with another in their pain' – walks with us all the way.

I find comfort in the experience of G W Hughes SJ as re-counted in his book God, Where Are You? He had lost two sisters to suicide, but in imagination he gradually became able to converse

*with them and with the rest of his family who had died — informal
chats based on the belief that they knew how things were for him,
and were interested in him; delighted when he was glad, supportive
when he was sad. He describes them as being like shy persons at
a party, who open up wonderfully when you engage with them.
This makes sense to me and I now believe that for God there are
no dead persons: 'God is God of the living, not the dead' (Luke
20:38). My sister-in-law has not fallen into the outer darkness of
nothingness; she is alive and well, more so than she ever was in this
life, and I look forward to meeting her again in God's due time and
continuing my conversations with her.*

For more on the fall-out from suicide, you might read: Brendan
McManus SJ *Surviving Suicide Bereavement: Finding Life After Death.*

FOR REFLECTION

We have all gone through experiences of being let down or betrayed.
Revisit some of your memories of such events. Over time how have
you come to terms with your pain? Has anything good emerged from
it for you?

EVIL UNDER THE MICROSCOPE

It is time for us to analyse evil. We know it intimately by experience, as we live through genocides, terrorism, wars of aggression, Islamic State militancy, clerical child abuse, cheating, embezzlement, and the rape of the earth. But it remains impossible to explain.

Evil cannot be understood directly. The *consequence* of a bad action can be grasped only too clearly, but the evil hidden in the action is less obvious. Consider the Holocaust: it was the outcome of a decision to eliminate the Jews from Europe. The evil originated in Hitler's intention and it was ruthlessly followed through. What was wrong with Hitler's intention? Something was *missing* from it, which we can name as the element of right reason. His intention was carefully thought out but unreasonable, radically unjust. Hitler took no account of the rights and dignity of his victims. *The core of evil is the absence of a reasonableness that should be present in a decision.* When we fail to act in accordance with reason, evil creeps in. And since there is something critical *missing* in what we call evil, we cannot hope to understand it well: it lacks essential meaning.

Punctures and Engines

Evil is an instance of failure in the moral order: the *failure* of reasonableness. We can call it a failure because something is absent which should be present, and the absence is someone's fault. To use a homely example: evil is a bit like the puncture in a tyre – something's missing that should be there! But what is a puncture? It's not a thing in itself. We can't gather punctures into boxes and analyse them! But they're real enough, as you know when you get one. Again, when the car won't start, it is because of *a failure* within the connections that make up the ignition process. We have no box for such failures, but again they are enormously real.

While punctures and seized-up engines are 'bad news', they are not moral evils. Moral evil occurs when *something is missing that should be present in our decision making.* It's a failure in the relationships between human beings. Rationality and reason are missing. Suppose a child angers his dad: the father hits the child across the face, then hits him again when he screams in shock and pain. This moment of domestic violence is a snapshot of evil: the father has acted irrationally. He has *'lost his reason'* for a moment. He might cool down after a bit and say *'I don't know what made me do that!'* The incident spoils the good relationship between parent and child, and casts a gloom over the home unless the dad apologises and in some way bridges the gap that he has created.

Evil Is Warped

We are meant to be reasonable beings, to act according to conscience. But we fail occasionally and do what we know is unreasonable. Evil is primarily in the *intention* rather than in the action itself. Thus, a surgical intervention brings pain to a patient, but the surgeon is acting to restore the patient's health. This justifies the pain caused. Muggers, on the other hand, inflict damage on their victims to get at their money. The former action is good because of the good intention, whereas the latter action is evil because of the unreasonable intention. Evil is the misuse of free will. Theologians had a cryptic formula to define evil: it is the absence of a good that should be present. That absent good is reasonableness, which should characterise all human interactions.

For something to be good, all relevant aspects have to be integrated. Contrary-wise, for something to be bad, a single defect is enough. In one way, the dice is stacked against the good: one disruptive neighbour is enough for a whole apartment block to have a sleepless night! For this reason we should not be too shocked at the occurrence of what is bad.

Evil brings a warp, a twist in the way things are meant to be. When we study it, something important is missing, so it cannot be understood directly. Evil can only be grasped indirectly and partially. No amount of poking or analysis can yield up the reasonableness that is missing. We need to face evil as calmly as we can and direct our energy into damage limitation.

Evil is tough, smart, elusive and durable. It can out-manoeuvre human solutions. Can it outwit even the divine response? That is the drama we are exploring!

Is Evil God's Fault?

In his book, *Is God to Blame?* G J Hughes points up aspects of the complexity hidden in that little word 'evil'.

Working from the viewpoint of philosophy – what we can know from reason alone – he says that a person can only be blamed as causing evil if each of the following conditions is met:

i) The action done is evil, all things considered.

ii) The person knew what they were doing and how things would turn out.

iii) The person could have done better.

iv) The person knew that they could have done better.

Let us reflect on these points first in a human situation, and then in relation to God.

Suicide Bombers

Suicide bombings offer dramatic instances of evil. But where does the evil come from? Recent profiles of suicide bombers reveal that often they are male, young adults, single, but not psychotic nor suicidal nor innately violent. They may be students. They may have no religious affiliation or they may defend their intention by asserting, '*It is the will of God*' and may see their action as a ticket to heaven. They take on their role freely and some may need only a few weeks of induction to become radicalised. They can apparently more easily be recruited from among young people with Asperger's Syndrome, whose capacity for relationship is below the norm.

Motivation

What motivates them to die in order to kill? They often see themselves as freedom fighters, martyrs for their cause. They may be seeking revenge for some traumatic event such as the slaughter of their own family; others hope that their dramatic intervention and self-sacrifice will stop future massacres.

Controlled experiments reveal that perhaps there lurks a suicide bomber in each of us; given the cluster of conditions that intending suicide bombers experience, might we do as they did? Would we say we were doing a moral wrong? After all, soldiers at war hope to kill as many of the enemy as possible. We honour those who kill in order to defend their country against aggression.

So, looking at our four conditions, we would say firstly that the action of suicide bombers is bad, even if they have a good intention. Secondly, they proceed, knowing what will happen. But on the third and fourth conditions, do they believe, in their particular surroundings, that they could do better? It appears not, given the testimony of some who have been caught before they could mount their attack.

My intention here is not to present an exhaustive analysis of the motivations of suicide bombers but to indicate the complexity of evil. It is many-layered.

Following on this, let us look for a moment at the death of Jesus. Whom should we blame? Jesus' intention is good: he accepts for the sake of humankind the death that is thrust on him. So we don't blame him. As for those who killed him, the soldiers were simply doing their job, obeying the order issued that Friday morning to crucify three criminals. How guilty were they? As for the members of the Sanhedrin, they decided that for the good of the nation, one man must die (see John 11:50). But are they guilty if, as Jesus says, they did not know what they were doing? And add in the fact that they certainly did not know how things would turn out! So who in your view was to blame?

This exercise makes us cautious about blaming! It provides the perspective we need to address our issue, '*Is God to blame when evil occurs?*' To this we now return.

Guilty as charged?

Should God be blamed for evil? Can it be shown that this world of ours is a bad one, *all things considered*? Hardly. In fact, it can be argued that from a philosophical point of view this may be as good a world as can be had. We do not have another universe built on similar lines with which to compare ours. Next, our world has much good about it, as well as having evil mixed in. When something that is good gets spoiled, but not spoiled through and through, then the question is, 'Can it be salvaged?' We can imagine God asking that very question and deciding in the affirmative, '*Yes, every last detail can and will be salvaged. Nothing will be lost!*'

We can blame God if in creating the world
- ♡ God doesn't know what will happen, or
- ♡ God knows about the evil that is going on and chooses to do nothing about it, or
- ♡ God knows about the evil but is unable to help. Recall the humorous line, '*God is alive and well, but working on a less ambitious project!*' Is this the case?

But on the other hand
- ♡ If God creates a good world and cares about it, and
- ♡ If the evil in the world comes not from God but from us, and

☙ If God engages decisively and radically with evil,
and

☙ If God manages to bring great good out of evil…

… then we are forced to search for some other reason to blame God for evil, or else must we say that God is innocent and not to blame for the miasma of evil?

Is Freedom a Bad Mistake?

We defined evil as the misuse of human freedom: from it most of the world's woes emerge. Hitler, Stalin, Pol Pot and an endless litany of infamous names come to mind. We looked at our experience of suffering at the hands of others and also noted the dark pages which contain the suffering we inflict in our turn. Would we be better off without freedom? Yet we think of freedom as one of our most precious gifts: it is what makes us unique, and through it extraordinary good is done: think no further than parents who freely love their children. We would not want to forego freedom, even though we would like to curb the freedom of wrongdoers. So is it reasonable to blame God for the evil resulting from the misuse of freedom? Of course we can say that God should not have made a world in which we can do wrong and that creation as we have it was a bad idea. But is God to blame if we do wrong? It is hard to prove that freedom is so wayward that it should have been omitted from the human make-up.

Is the Effort to Salvage Human History Worthwhile?

Here is where reason needs faith to carry our search along. Faith offers a vision which reason alone cannot attain. It is common to think of faith as a leap into the dark, but it is more enriching to think of it as turning the light on in a dark room. The simple but fundamental question, *'Who am I?'* can yield minimally satisfying answers if a person has no religious belief: *'You're born; you suffer; you die. End of story.'* Marxism would assert that persons are of economic value only

41

– mere cogs in the machine of progress. Faith however opens up new and breath-taking words about who I am: '*I am made in God's image; I am infinitely loved by God; God has taken on my human condition and given new meaning to my suffering and death; and I am destined to share eternal life with God*'. Which answer is better?

Faith brings light and expansiveness if I choose to accept it. But is it true? Are statements based on faith to be trusted? All depends on the basis for the belief. While erroneous beliefs abound, certain beliefs can be shown to be reasonable. From the beginning, Christians have been challenged *to offer a reason for the faith that is in them* (1 Peter 3:15). They have responded for twenty centuries and will continue to do so, not out of stubbornness but because they judge that the evidence for their belief can stand up to any argument. In the context of Christian belief about the wonder and destiny of the human person, it makes sense to affirm that the effort to salvage human history is worthwhile, and that the divine investment in the wellbeing of humankind can succeed. For in the Christian tradition God enters our world in Jesus Christ, opposes evil in all its forms, and experiences it personally to the point of death. Jesus brings a seismic shift to our human understanding of evil and suffering. His resurrection shows to the believer that love overcomes evil and death. This grounds Christian hope that evil has been radically mastered, even if it still ravages the earth and continues to break human hearts.

Thomas Merton in *Conjectures of a Guilty Bystander* speaks of the wonder of the human person as seen through God's eyes. Something happened for him as he was doing the shopping for his monastery in Louisville, Kentucky, on the corner of Fourth and Walnut. He was gazing at the other shoppers on the Mall.

PURE DIAMOND

Then it was as if I suddenly saw the secret beauty of their hearts, the depths of their hearts where neither sin nor desire nor self-knowledge can reach, the core of their reality, the person that each one is in God's eyes.

If only they could all see themselves as they really are. If only we could see each other that way all the time. There would be no more war, no more hatred, no more greed... I suppose the big problem would be that we would fall down and worship each other. But this cannot be seen, only believed and understood by a peculiar gift.

At the centre of our being is a point of nothingness which is untouched by sin and by illusion, a point of pure truth which belongs entirely to God, from which God disposes of our lives, which is inaccessible to the fantasies of our own mind or the brutalities of our own will.

This little point of nothingness and of absolute poverty is the pure glory of God in us. It is like a pure diamond, blazing with the invisible light of heaven. It is in everybody and if we could see it we would see these billions of points of life coming together in the face and blaze of a sun that would make all the darkness and cruelty of life vanish completely.

FOR REFLECTION

How do you see yourself? Do Merton's insights touch your heart? Have you ever had a moment such as he had, when the veil was lifted and you saw into the mystery of humanity in a deeper way than before?

IS SUFFERING GOD'S FAULT?

We have proposed that God is not to blame for evil in the world. Moral evil is the consequence of human unreasonableness. But what about physical or 'natural' suffering; sicknesses, diseases, famines, droughts, death? Is God to blame here?

By deciding to create our sort of world, God is responsible for the suffering that comes to us as vulnerable beings. Made of flesh and blood, we will die; we live in a carnivorous world in which creatures – including ourselves – kill other innocent creatures to stay alive; thousands of people are suddenly swept to their deaths by the convulsions of the earth in tsunamis and earthquakes. It seems that this is how an evolving planet must behave, but our advice was not asked about the world God has created! Could God have made a world with all the fragile beauty of this one, but without its vulnerability to suffering? We do not know. Suffering is inbuilt in our creation, and to be human is to suffer. But does God also send us some tailor-made sufferings?

The author of the *Letter to the Hebrews* wants to strengthen his readers to endure whatever sufferings come their way, and the first Christians endured such in plenty. He images God as a concerned parent who dispenses suffering as a discipline for our good. Christ himself, we are told, was *'made perfect through suffering'* and so it will be with us. Painful at the time, suffering is valuable in the long run and brings patience and courage. But is suffering a set-up job, prepared for us by God, or does God rather *make use* of the suffering which is inbuilt into being human, and help us to draw good from it? It would seem so.

That suffering can help us to grow is an enduring theme in great literature. *'Sweet are the uses of adversity'* is Shakespeare's summary in *As You Like It*. Self-knowledge and growth in humility come at a price: it is painful to have to abandon our cherished illusions in order to live

44

in the truth that sets us free (John 8:32). Pope Paul VI sums up a rich tradition in noting that *'There are things one can see only with eyes that have wept'*.

Suffering can mature us and bring us to levels of development that we might not otherwise reach. The stories in these pages abundantly illustrate this point. It is within parameters such as these we make our way gingerly along in trying to understand how God acts in our lives. Perhaps, as the graduate said on receiving her doctorate, *'Now, after seven years of study, I am still confused, but on a higher level!'*

The central point to keep in mind is that *'God is always working for our good'* (Rom 8:28). This includes the challenge to bring good from evil. In Christian understanding, God loves us, always wishes us well and works in all things for our lasting good. God uses the suffering that is inbuilt into created reality to open our hearts towards unrestricted loving. Our hearts are indeed broken open, but only that we may become free.

Nature in Distress

Does human evil upset the delicate balances of nature? If we imagine that creation and ourselves are qualitatively distinct, then we will find no link between human sin and the suffering of nature. But if, as science shows, we are interwoven with the rest of creation, the links between what we do and what emerges in nature become more obvious. As Pope Francis' encyclical *Laudato Si* (2015) says, nature groans in protest at our greed and insensitivity as we turn our world into a rubbish dump and our seas into cemeteries.

The early biblical authors had a parallel insight. They had their own sense of the dynamic unity of created reality but they put it in theological terms, since they were talking about God and God's relationship with humankind. They say that by usurping the place of God and deciding for ourselves how we would live, we betrayed what was entrusted to us, so relationships began to fall apart. Before the Fall nature is shown as being submissive to humans; animals are brought to Adam to name; everything is good, very good (Genesis 1:31). After the Fall, however, nature is experienced as cursed and hostile to humankind. Fruitful earth comes to yield only thorns and thistles; woman's pain in childbearing increases; her domination by man begins; and death enters the world (Genesis 3:14-19).

Although sin is *interior* to us and comes from the heart, its effects are seen *outwardly* in the disharmony of our bodies. Inner death is revealed by outer death; inner decay seeps out. So the warp of sin elaborated in Genesis has its repercussions in the material universe. The disorder brought by sin infects creation, according to St Paul (Romans 8:19-22). Only in a restored universe will creation, currently subject to decay, obtain *'the freedom of the children of God'* (8:21). The restoration of humankind to its original glory will encompass all of creation. What was disfigured will be restored to its divinely established beauty. In the new heavens and earth, sin, suffering and death will be definitively undone (Rev 21:1-5). In the meantime, the universe is caught up in a painful childbirth (Rom 8:19). But according to the authors of the *Dictionary of Biblical Theology* '*the total sweep of scripture invites the hope that a redeemed and freed creation will forever remain the world of God's children gathered together in Christ'*. It is a comfort, when we are dismayed by the ruin of what is beautiful in nature, to know that God's creative word can restore everything to its original glory.

Blame Satan?

Although not mentioned in the Creeds, the Church has taken Satan's existence for granted, following the many indications of scripture and Jesus' own comments on the personal powers of darkness. The elements of evil include the darkness that obscures good decision making; the experience of being tugged in ways which at our best we do not want to travel; the fact that people spoil life for others by acting unreasonably, and the experience that so many things go wrong for us – such elements can easily be gathered together and personalised into a demonic figure. People say, '*The devil made me do it!*' Or '*The Bad Guy really has it in for me!*'

Many people today discredit the notion of evil spirits as outmoded myth. Scripture scholars such as Walter Wink, who has studied the '*principalities and powers*' of the New Testament in depth, advise that our concern should focus on the concrete systems and institutions which bring structural evil into our world, rather than on the '*powers*' in the heavens. He attacks institutions such as multi-national corporations, banks and armies which create a certain sort of good, but are essentially self-serving and so bring disaster to those who stand in their way. Witness the greed and the collapse of commercial banks over the past decade, and the trail of misery they leave behind them. Harvey Cox notes how we tend to lay the blame for evil on others rather than on ourselves. His book *On Not Leaving It to the Snake*, argues for the importance of our choices. Even not to decide is to decide. To say '*I didn't do anything!*' seems like a statement of innocence, but it may be a statement of guilt – I did not do what I could and should have done. Jesus makes the same point: '*You didn't feed me when I was hungry*' (Matthew 25:42): by doing nothing in the face of the needs of others we miss the whole point about human living, which is the fostering of good relationships. To blame Satan for the suffering of the world is to deny our own role in it.

Could God Do Better?

Some time ago the son of a friend of mine contracted cancer. The mother rallied a wide web of people to pray for his cure. He had a happy family who depended on him, but he died in his thirties. We had indeed prayed, but the heavens were silent. Why didn't God intervene in this and innumerable other situations? One member of the family said to me, *'I think God is a non-interventionist, and a god who turns away from human pain is not worth having!'*

God certainly does not intervene as we would like. The cures reported in the Gospels, the promises of Jesus about our prayer being heard – all these can become meaningless when no cure is forthcoming for the person I love. I have no satisfactory explanation for such stony silence. I don't believe that the plans of God are so rigidly in place that no intervention is allowed. I think of miracles and wonder why they cannot be more frequent. My recurring question for God is: *'Why do you allow such pain, such cruel breaking of human hearts?'*

God, Are You There?

So I have had to face the fact that God is vastly different from me: if I were God I'd respond to people's petitions: I'd comfort sufferers and stop their tears. I'd do what Jesus did: *'He cured all who were sick'* (Matthew 8:16)! So I have been forced to wrestle with my images of God and move away from the notion that life should be a cosy affair from which sickness and suffering are absent. I have had to accommodate myself to the fact that God's thinking and God's ways are infinitely beyond me. As Job was reduced to silence before God, so often am I.

God is total Mystery to us and does not answer most of our *'Why?'* questions in regard to suffering. God's thoughts are not ours (Isaiah 55:8-9). We do not understand why God should create a universe racked by so much suffering. How can a good God watch the agonies of those whom he professes to love? Nor again do we understand how God can think it worthwhile to labour throughout human history to resolve the ravages of suffering and evil.

Is God Good?

The notion of God as a 'non-interventionist' is current in some circles, hence the popular image of God as the great clock-maker in the sky who makes a beautiful instrument, winds it up and then stands back, letting it slowly run down. But the Hebrews did not see God as a non-interventionist. Their religion was based on a deep sense of the great deeds of God in their lives and history. They got this conviction not from some philosophical theory but simply by looking around them and by reflecting on their extraordinary history.

Creation, they felt, was so wonderful, so well-arranged and at their service that its Author must be good. Imagine yourself having a meal with a Hebrew family on a cool evening some 2,500 years ago. To make conversation you ask, '*Why do the Hebrews believe that God is good?*' They might wave their hands to the moon or the stars and say, '*God brings everything into existence, and existence is good. It is good to be alive! Life is good! Come on, have more wine, or some pomegranate!*' They had no doubts about stating that '*God saw everything that he had made, and indeed, it was very good*' (Genesis 1:31). The little word '*good*' recurs 906 times in the Bible, and often in reference to God. They praised God's great deeds, of which creation was the most obvious: there it is, all around – earth in all its wonder, the sun, moon and stars. The sheer goodness and magnificence of things proclaims God's steadfast love and goodness (Psalm 136).

Laudato Si

We can learn from the Hebrews who are our religious ancestors. The goodness of our disfigured creation is becoming more precious to us today – the recent encyclical letter of Pope Francis, *Laudato Si*, invites us to respect creation which reveals the goodness of God. All creation is precious; God's goodness overflows to us in everything created. Our lives depend on the constancy and order of nature. While things occasionally go wrong, the overall goodness of reality underlies everything – it's the way the world is made! The psalmist attributes such goodness to God: '*You crown the year with your goodness*' (Psalm 65:11). So from the goodness of creation we can reasonably hold that God is good; likewise goodness abounds in so many persons across the world, including yourself. There is a quiet love which holds things together, especially in hard times. Where does all that goodness and that love come from, if not from God?

God's Saving Interventions

In responding further to the question, 'Is God good?' the Hebrews would refer to their own epic story – how God chose and guided them down the years. They had been nomads, and then slaves; they had been mysteriously liberated, and arrived after great toil and pain in a land '*flowing with milk and honey*' – but they hadn't made this new land fruitful, nor had they got there under their own steam! They knew that it was God who had brought them there, and prepared this home for them. And this was done not because they were great people, but simply because God loved them.

To give themselves hope and trust in difficult times they clung to their belief in the goodness of God. They recalled endlessly 'the great deeds of God' and had the sense that God was '*on their side, a mighty hero*' (Isaiah 42:13).

From the Christian perspective, as we shall see, God is still doing mighty deeds and shaping history for our good. The greatest deed of God is the redemption of the world through the life, death and resurrection of Jesus, which underpins Christian belief that God acts decisively and effectively to resolve evil and suffering.

The final great deed of God will be the Parousia – God's glorious return at the close of human history. It will reveal to the people of all time God's total victory over evil: this is the theme of the *Book of Revelation*.

Could God do better? Does it now seem reasonable to hold that

God is good, despite the dark presence of suffering and evil in the world?

If indeed God intervenes in human affairs, the following story hints that God is asking us also to be interventionists in whatever ways we can.

STRENGTH AND COURAGE: MALALA

'Let us pick up our books and our pens'. So said Malala Yousafzai in her address to young leaders from 100 countries at the United Nations Youth Assembly in New York, in 2014. 'They are our most powerful weapons. One child, one teacher, one book, and one pen can change the world. Education is the only solution.'

Ms Yousafzai, wearing a shawl that had once belonged to Benazir Bhutto who was assassinated in Pakistan in 2007, spoke in a calm, self-assured voice. It was her first major speech since she was shot in the head on her way home from school in Pakistan's Swat Valley. She recalled how the attackers had also shot her friends.

'They thought that the bullets would silence us,' she said, 'but they were wrong. Out of that silence came thousands of voices. The terrorists thought that they would change our aims and stop our ambitions but nothing changed in my life except that my weakness, fear and hopelessness died. Strength, power and courage were born. I am the same Malala. My ambitions are the same. My hopes are the same. My dreams are the same.'

FOR REFLECTION

Is God responsible for Malala's horrific experience? How do you think God invites you to engage in the struggle for human dignity? What were Malala's resources, and what are yours?

PART TWO:
IS SOMETHING GOOD GOING ON?

IS GOD WATCHING OUT FOR OUR HAPPINESS?

Suffering and evil raise issues which will not go away. One of them concerns what we call 'Providence'. The other concerns God's care for our happiness. Does Providence work, and if so, how? Is God watching out for our happiness, and if so why do we have to endure so much?

Is God Provident?

My father worked for forty-seven years as a clerk on the railway. He earned a tiny salary for long days of work, and spent very little on himself. My mother and he did what they could to care for their small family, but all sorts of things lay outside their control and limited their possibilities. Life in Ireland in the middle decades of the last century did not foster imagination and initiative. So as a family we lived not far from the poverty-line; treats were few and carefully budgeted for; opportunities to explore a wider world were very limited; a conservative Church dominated our inner landscape with its narrow focus on the pitfalls leading to eternal damnation.

Now, is God like a well-intentioned father who does his best to provide for his family but often fails due to lack of resources or the interference of others? Or is divine providence comprehensive, like comprehensive insurance but without 'terms and conditions'? The world is littered with good plans which don't work out because unforeseeable factors enter in and wreck them, or the goodwill to execute them is in short supply. Think only of failed efforts by the United Nations to eliminate malaria or to provide clean water for everyone; think of Malala's determination to enable the children of the world to access education. Is divine providence like that, well-intentioned but in all likelihood doomed to frustration?

Everything Under Control?

My parents had to deal with the world they found before them in the late 1930s. They accommodated as best they could to its ever-changing contours. The Second World War broke out shortly after they married: it changed the face of Europe and the lives of its people. My parents' planning was therefore always provisional. So when my father died of cancer his pension was cut off immediately, leaving my mother to fend for herself for almost twenty years until a widow's pension was provided.

Recall your own efforts to shape a good and happy life and the factors that cut across it every so often. Does God's freedom also get upset by outside events?

We do not well understand how God goes about things. But the following points give hints as to why we can reasonably say that God is provident and that this providence is effective in a way that human providence cannot be.

> ☙ Divine planning is different from ours: God does not firstly create and then decide what to do with what is created. God goes at things the other way round. In other words God first *plans* everything and then creates in view of the plan. This is what it means to say that God is the lord of history. With appropriate control of all relevant factors, the divine plan can be successful. Our bad choices do not dismay God. There may be glitches, but they are not unexpected.

🐦 Everything that God sets up is *good,* simply because God is good. So we can say that God's planning is spacious, not restricted; it extends across the board and takes all elements into account, including the aberrations that we humans bring to the plot of human history. For us, a lightning transport strike disrupts the best of plans: everyone has to walk, cycle or drive to work, leading to chaos for those on the move. But for God there are *no unforeseen events* which can create chaos in the divine project, though they require God, as it were, to work harder and dig deeper into divine resources. Divine planning doesn't get caught out. God plans comprehensively, taking *everything* into account, including human failure and the failures that occur in nature.

🐦 We have to work within the limits created by time and space and the slow unfolding of human history, with all its unpredictable ups and downs. But God is free of time and space and history – these belong to the human world, not to the divine. We learn slowly over a lifetime, and we learn only a little about reality; but in God there is no guess-work: God has it 'all together' always. God does not make mistakes.

🐦 To say, however, that God is provident does not mean that nothing will ever go wrong for us. God is not running a celestial Welfare State in which all our needs are catered for. Tsunamis of disaster occur in our world. The sheep in Psalm 23 finds itself in the valley of darkness! The basic meaning of the word *provident* is 'to look out for'. The shepherd looks out for his sheep in the valley and guides it through all dangers. God does likewise for us, supporting us along difficult paths, while challenging us to use the resources with which we are providentially supplied.

❦ Has God then got 'everything under control'? This is not a helpful phrase in our context: God prefers nuanced control rather than absolute control, which would eliminate human freedom. A later chapter, 'How God works in our lives', will explore the balance between God's freedom and ours. Here it may be enough to use the image of God as a good school principal who runs a large school effectively, while respecting the uniqueness and freedom of each teacher and student. Glitches occur but the principal gets around them.

Does God Intend Us to be Happy?

Before reading further, take a few moments to explore the quality of your own happiness. Are you happy, or at least content? What is it that makes you so? What eats into your happiness?

We are beings who desire happiness, and we go to great trouble to find it. I like gardening: I plant crocus and snowdrop bulbs so that the flowers will give me joy in early spring. Workers toil for long hours in order to enjoy themselves in their free time. Parents go to trouble to bring their families to the beach, hoping for a sunny day. Armies march into battle because they believe that through the defeat of the enemy they – or at least their loved ones – will have happiness.

We spend our lives reaching out toward what makes for happiness. The desire for happiness gets us out of bed each morning! Hope sustains us as we pursue objectives that are hard to attain. Suffering comes in here, but it seems worthwhile. For the vast majority of people, to be alive is a good thing. We tend to dread old age, because it diminishes happiness: techniques to stave off the unhappiness of decline and death are a multi-billion business.

Secure Happiness

We want happiness and spontaneously believe we have a right to it. This is why suffering can seem so wrong. Security in happiness would mean an end to evil and suffering. Now is this what the Creator has in mind for us? If the Greek gods had no concern for the happiness of humankind, is the God of Jewish and Christian tradition any different? Or are we set up to be denied what we most desire? Is God 'winding us up'? Is human happiness only to be fragile and occasional, or can we hope like St Paul that *the sufferings of this present time are not worth comparing with the glory about to be revealed to us'* (Romans 8:18). Are we perhaps programmed for a lasting happiness that will make us forget our former woes?

God and Our Happiness

We have presented the case for the goodness of God. Now we can propose that God's goodness and our happiness in fact meet together. Because God is good and also happy, God creates us for happiness and programmes into us our desire for it. Of course God's problem is to get us to learn where true happiness lies. We are slow pupils. Happiness for believers lies in knowing that they are infinitely loved by God, and in their responding by loving God, other people, themselves and creation in return. Happiness for non-believers is less focussed and less satisfying. Jesus uses the image of merchants searching for fine pearls; if they are fortunate to stumble on one, they sell all to buy it. The Athenians to whom St Paul spoke were also searching for a lasting happiness: they had an altar *'to an Unknown God'*. Why God does not enable everyone to find the real God in the course of their lifetime is, however, another issue for me to put in my imaginary little book titled *'Must Ask God About That.'*

According as we deepen our relationship with God, we move closer to 'home'. Our homeward path, however, is a rocky one due to our waywardness. But God is on our side always, prompting, pushing and drawing us forward. As we shall see, divine goodness stretches to extraordinary lengths to ensure that we finally come to eternal happiness.

Not the Whole Story?

But what then about evil? Because of media coverage our generation is more aware of the magnitude of human suffering than any previous one. If we say that God is good and works for our happiness, what of the endless stream of things that make life hard for us? In response we have to go back to our arguments for the goodness and providence of God, and to God's interventions in history. We are given hints of how God works to outwit evil, but until the drama of human history is complete, the awesome scope of divine planning will be hidden from us.

So when someone asks, *'How can you say God is good when so many disasters happen?'* you must cling to the belief that God is good, even if you can't convince them of this fact. Both Hebrews and early Christians insisted on the goodness of God, of life, of existence, despite all difficulties. These people were not fools. This conviction leads to praise and gratitude in the Psalms, and later in the Christian Eucharist. The liturgy states that despite all that goes wrong and is not yet sorted out, it is right *always and everywhere* to give thanks for all that God does for us. It is as if the Christian community is saying: *'OK, endless things happen to cause us pain. This world is far from perfect. But look, the big elements in our happiness are in place – creation is awesome; the incarnation means that God is fully on our side; God is looking after the problems of sin, evil and even death; God cares personally for all and each of us, and our long-range future is guaranteed. Don't sweat the small stuff. Don't fixate on the imperfection of things or the fact that God seems to take ages to get his act fully together!'*

If we have a weak sense of the radical goodness of the cosmos, it is hard for us to stand up to evil. This is why I find it important to keep in close touch with nature in its quiet dependability and beauty. Creation is the first and the ongoing revelation of the goodness and wonder of God, and anchored in this I can more adequately face things that go wrong. I also need good friends, people who are coping reasonably well with life's downturns. I am coming more and more to notice in ordinary lives a quiet goodness in face of evil. On a humble and daily level, I can look at the massive care provided by parents which enables children to trust that the world can be a safe and welcoming place. Such parents are teaching their families in concrete ways that we live in a friendly rather than a hostile universe.

The core message of the New Testament is *victory*. It is a dramatic scenario of how God will sort out the evil of the world and bring peace and joy to humankind. Victory, we are told, is radically won: there remain only the mopping up operations. We have our part to play here. But while in our thinking victory for one side means defeat for another, the New Testament message is that all humankind, beyond expectations and imaginings, is invited to the victory celebrations. No need then to sweat the small stuff: with sin and evil radically overcome, death yields to resurrection, love triumphs, and there is hope for the salvation of all. In all of this the goodness of God shines out, and God's provident care for our happiness. We need to keep the grand scenario in view, else we will get fixated on the black spots. Our desire for a perfect world will be met only when all is transfigured. In this world many things are good: don't let perfectionism eclipse that fact.

SALVATION IS THROUGH LOVE

Man's Search For Meaning, by Viktor Frankl, is a classic tribute to hope from the Holocaust. He tells how he was brought to an awareness that something lies beyond suffering and evil: it is love.

> *As a prisoner-of-war in a Nazi concentration camp he endured forced marches in the depths of winter: stumbling along the frozen paths, the guards kept shouting and driving the prisoners with the butts of their rifles. The icy wind did not encourage talk, but the man next to him whispered suddenly, 'If our wives could see us now!' They stumbled on; nothing was said, but each of them was thinking of his wife. Frankl heard her answering him, saw her smile, her frank and encouraging look. Her look was then more luminous than the sun which was beginning to rise. For the first time in his life, he says, he saw the truth – that love is the ultimate and the highest goal to which we can aspire. He grasped the meaning of the greatest secret that poetry and belief have to impart: that the salvation of humankind is through love and in love. Had he known then that his wife was dead, he asserts that his mental conversation with her would have been just as vivid and satisfying, for love, as the Song of Songs affirmed long ago, is as strong as death: nothing could touch the strength of his love, his thoughts, and the image of his beloved.*

FOR REFLECTION

In an appalling setting the author comes to a profound insight about the mystery of love and goodness. How does his insight sit with you? Have you ever found yourself at the end of your lifeline, only to stumble on the conviction that love alone matters? Name for yourself what keeps you going in difficult times.

A WOMAN TALKS WITH GOD ABOUT EVIL

I said in the previous chapter that we get hints of how God may be working in the depths of suffering and evil. It is good to muse over concrete instances. Viktor Frankl's moment of illumination – that love is our ultimate and highest goal, and that it is the heartbeat of the universe – occurred near Auschwitz during the Holocaust in the Second World War. He survived the Nazi persecution and lived on till 1997. By contrast, Etty Hillesum was a Jew who lived in Holland between two World Wars. Intelligent and gifted, she became caught up in helping the Jews who were being expelled from Holland in 1942, and worked in Westerbork, a transit camp which led to Auschwitz and to extermination. Fear and misery were the essence of the camp, yet in this hell she wrote, *'Despite everything, life is full of beauty and meaning.'* Her shining personality and ability to read human hearts helped many Jews to endure the horrors of Westerbork. She later determined to share the fate of her family and fellow Jews and on the train for Auschwitz she threw a postcard out the window which was found by farmers. It had the line which expressed her soul: *'We left the camp singing.'* They reached Auschwitz on 10 September 1943, and that very day her mother and father were gassed. She herself suffered the same fate in November, aged 29. The final sentence of her diaries reads: *'We should be willing to act as a balm for all wounds.'* That was how she had lived. A friend described her life as 'a marvellous gift'.

Her Inner Journey

Etty's astonishing internal journey echoes classical accounts of spiritual transformation. Capable though she was of extroversion and engagement, her most intense need, and gift, was for the inner life. Her essential development took place in the privacy of self-reflection. Her diary is a constant drive toward personal honesty. She knew how to follow the subtle movements of her feelings and how to question and criticise herself. *'My protracted headaches are so much masochism; my abundant compassion is so much self-gratification.'*

As her tenderness and detachment deepened, she reported in her diary a new serenity, a steady sense of identity. She had the courage to follow the thread of her own experience. She began to describe states which we identify as religious: gratitude for all that was given to her, a profound self-acceptance and acceptance of others, a conviction of the inward beauty and rightness of life, no matter how appalling it was on the outside. She came to a place where she could feel the hidden harmony of the world.

In the last stages of her amazing journey she seemed to attain that peace that passes understanding. She drew sustenance from reading and musing, and from savouring moments of beauty and quiet: the glorious blue sky, the field of purple lupins, the moonlight 'made of silver and eternity'. She had a sense of the majestic stream of life, which includes within itself pain and suffering as well as happiness and joy, and which has to be accepted in all its encompassing depths. She believed that the microcosm of the soul can encompass the external world and, in addition, hold infinite space. Her level of intimacy with God was that of a mystic.

Forgiveness and Peace

But she was practical and ruthlessly honest with herself. She was convinced that it was her vocation and everyone's duty to look first to themselves and solve the war within. In her diary she wrote, *'We have so much work to do on ourselves that we shouldn't even be thinking of hating our so-called enemies. We are hurtful enough to one another as it is. Each of us must turn inward and destroy in ourselves all that we think we ought to destroy in others. And remember that every atom of hate we add to this world makes it still more inhospitable. But that is nothing but Christianity!'* Etty in fact remained a Jew until her death, though she drew inspiration from the Gospels.

'YOU CANNOT HELP US!'

The following lines give a hint of the depth of her relationship with God:

> *Dear God, these are anxious times. Tonight for the first time I lay in the dark with burning eyes as scene after scene of human suffering passed before me. I shall promise You one thing, God, just one very small thing: I shall never burden my today with cares about tomorrow, although that takes some practice. Each day is sufficient unto itself. I shall try to help You, God, to stop my strength ebbing away, though I cannot vouch for it in advance. But one thing is becoming increasingly clear to me: that You cannot help us, that we must help You to help ourselves. And that is all we can manage these days and also all that really matters: that we safeguard that little piece of You, God, in ourselves. And perhaps in others as well. Alas, there doesn't seem to be much You Yourself can do about our circumstances, about our lives. Neither do I hold You responsible. You cannot help us, but we must help You and defend Your dwelling place inside us to the last.*

Was Etty right in saying that God was unable to help as the Holocaust went on? Certainly God did not intervene directly: God respected the freedom of the Nazis, even at its worst. God's 'help' was of a different order, but it was intensely real: nothing less than God can explain how Etty kept going in her impossible circumstances. God, she believed, was indeed intervening through her, helping her to keep the flame of care and love alive in a world of horror.

You can read more about this fascinating woman in Etty Hillesum: *An Interrupted Life and Letters From Westerbork.*

FOR REFLECTION

You probably know of people whose lives have been cut short before they could fulfil their potential. Etty died at 29. Yet her life reveals how a person may reach in those short years an extraordinary level of wisdom. How do her story and her message of forgiveness speak to you? Do you ever glimpse, even briefly, something of 'the hidden harmony of the world' that underlies evil?

OLD TESTAMENT INSIGHTS ON EVIL

The story of Etty Hillesum, brought up in the Jewish tradition, raises the question of how the Hebrews understood evil. It also highlights the startling freshness of the message of Jesus.

St John Paul II spoke of the Bible as *'The Book of Suffering.'* It is a startling title, but all too accurate. From the early pages of the *Book of Genesis* to the close of the *Book of Revelation*, suffering, evil and their resolution are the central theme. Many authors played their part in writing the different books of the Bible, and since each had their own view on these matters they often contradict one another and thereby confuse us!

Wipe Them Out?
Early Hebrew writers describe God as finding that since evil on earth is getting out of hand, the only remedy is to wipe away sinners and start again: hence the myth of the Flood and the destruction of Sodom and Gomorrah. But then out of love for humankind God 'repents' and promises not to repeat the Deluge. God is portrayed as having to think out a better strategy to cope with human waywardness! Such stories simply mirror how a well-intentioned human being would deal with evil, and are not to be taken literally.

Does God Cause Evil?
Other writers felt – reluctantly, no doubt – that they had to ascribe the authorship of evil to God. The Book of Job closes with God doubling the fortune of Job, *'after all the evil that the Lord had brought upon him'* (42:10-17). The authors of *Exodus* say that *'God hardened the heart of Pharaoh'* so that he would not let the Chosen People go. These writers were doing their best to defend the *omnipotence* of God: they could not allow the idea that there was an independent evil power over against

God; but then they were trapped into asserting that if God is the author of all reality, God must cause evil as well as good. So their inadequate interpretation of the nature of evil forced them to say that prior to the Exodus of the Hebrews from Egypt, it was God who hardened Pharaoh's heart, and that God sent the plagues which scourged the Egyptians, including the slaughter of their first-born, innocent animals included. We must beware of such literalism, and instead say that since evil is a failure in reasonableness, it is Pharaoh, not God, who is at fault.

In the New Testament itself, we get a hangover from Hebrew thinking. So St Paul asserts that God imprisons everyone in disobedience so that he may be merciful to all (Romans 11:32). But God, as the author of our freedom, does not imprison us, so this turn of phrase is again a biblical shorthand to indicate how God shapes human history for the good of all, and is not to be taken literally.

The *Book of Job* probes in depth the theme of God and evil. This fictional work portrays God as sending Job appalling suffering in order to prove his high quality. The theme of suffering as *merited punishment* is explored by his friends but Job maintains his innocence. At the end, Job meets the God of majesty. The plot now passes beyond the issue of guilt or innocence. The omnipotence and omniscience of God dominate, and poor Job ends up admitting that he does not know what he is talking about: the encounter with God renders him speechless.

Perhaps we can learn from this: when left to our own ways of thinking, our notions about evil are threadbare and flimsy. Only when we grasp something of God's project as revealed historically in Jesus, can we say something helpful about evil sorrow and pain.

Has God Enemies?

I worked in Northern Ireland towards the end of 'the Troubles' as they were quaintly called. The opposing sides had painted murals at the gable ends of their houses to give heart to their own followers and to instil fear into their enemies. One mural which chilled me included the text, *'When the Lord brings you into the land you are about to occupy and clears away many nations before you, then you must utterly destroy them. Show them no mercy'* (Deuteronomy 7:1-2). Small-minded people took this literally, with appalling results. Again the text must be seen as a well-intentioned but rather clumsy effort by biblical writers to justify their own wars and their ways of dealing with those who stood in their way. They shaped a god in the image and likeness of an earthly king. So Psalm 68 runs: *'Let God rise up, let his enemies be scattered... Let the wicked perish before God... God will shatter the heads of his enemies'.* God does not act so; but we have to wait for the New Testament to learn that God cares for everyone, including the bad. God in fact sees no-one as enemy: God does not remain neutral in human conflicts but acts for both sides to bring about reconciliation.

Why Do The Evil Prosper?

Given then that God does not *cause* evil, the sacred authors still had a problem: why do the evil prosper? They try to show that God defends good people from the wrongdoing of others. An early view was that God ensures that the innocent are spared suffering and evil. So the psalmist says, *'I have been young and now am old, yet I have not seen the righteous forsaken or their children begging bread'* (Psalm 37:25). There is a charming naivete about this reflection: one wonders in what world this ostrich-like figure was living!

A slightly more sophisticated view was that God does indeed allow the innocent to suffer at the hand of the wicked, but then rescues them. *'Many are the afflictions of the righteous, but the Lord rescues them from them all'* (Psalm 34:19). But it isn't so!

Some writers take the bull by the horns and ask God to do away with the wicked; and they offer blood-curdling advice on how God might go about it. *'Dear Lord, wake up and do to them what we would do if we were able, and do it now!'* But God does not oblige. The wicked prosper merrily; they appear blessed, not cursed. Where is God in this?

Justice Beyond Death

Only toward the end of the Old Testament did the Hebrews begin to entertain the idea that there must be a state *beyond death* in which justice will prevail. Then, they decided, God will finally *reward the good and punish the wicked*. Many of us today, brought up on the old Catechism, still accept this solution as the final state of things, and we find it in the Gospels. But while this interpretation of God's response to evil has seeped into Christian thought, it has to be jettisoned in the light of the full understanding of the work of Jesus. Don't blame the Old Testament writers: with their limited insight into divine thinking, they were doing their best. But again, don't live out of their explanations now that the New Testament is to hand! To stick with the Old Testament is like using an out of date phone list!

The *New* Testament is indeed new, and news is truly news when something runs sharply contrary to expectation. The Good News explodes our human ideas of how the drama of history will turn out. A great leap forward in the understanding of God's heart takes place in Jesus.

Incarnate Loving

As we shall see, Jesus offers in his own person the full interpretation of God's response to suffering and evil. This is the light that shines through what is otherwise impenetrable mystery. His message, shown in what he does and says, is that God is *simply* love; better still is to say that God is Pure Active Loving. This Loving which is at the heart of reality is love of an unique kind and it becomes totally vulnerable in the human person, Jesus. He is Incarnate Loving, which is shown not in power but in service. This Loving is so great as to include love of enemies, wrongdoers and sinners, as the Gospels attest. God intends *to save* the wicked, not to condemn them to eternal punishment. Evil will indeed be sorted out, but not by eliminating or punishing the wicked. It is to be integrated within God's all-embracing project of the salvation of all humankind. Later on we will explore the most fundamental of all questions: dare we hope then that all people will in fact be saved?

CELEBRATION IN BELSEN

An Irish Jesuit was sent as Chaplain to Belsen Concentration Camp as it was being liberated in 1945. The misery was beyond description: thousands dying of starvation, mounds of unburied dead. Affected for the rest of his life by what he saw and endured, he spoke little about it. He told one story however. He had planned a Mass – the first ever in Belsen – on a makeshift altar under the open sky. But when the day came there was torrential rain, and sitting in his little hut he thought of cancelling the Mass. When he got to the altar, however, he found hundreds of people lying or standing in the mud, waiting for him. Some were Christian, others Jewish, others had lost any religious affiliation. But there they were.

After that, Mass was celebrated there every day.

FOR REFLECTION

What do you honestly think should happen to evildoers? When you have answered that question ask yourself whether you have included or excluded yourself from this problematic group! How deeply do you accept that God's project is to bring everyone, bad and good, safely home to eternal joy? Have you a sense that this is the underlying drama of our times, and that you have an important part to play in it?

PART THREE:
GOD'S RADICAL RESPONSE TO EVIL

THE GOD OF JESUS CHRIST

The enduring question when evil occurs is, 'Can we still say that God is good?' We now come to the heart of the Christian response.

No Santa!

Mature trust in divine goodness is not like the belief we had about Santa Claus, that benevolent figure who goes to great trouble to make children happy, and is generous with his gifts. The myths of childhood must not be carried into our adult world, yet we may still have the image of God as a celestial Santa whose role is simply to make us happy by meeting our desires, wiping away our tears, and making all things well here and now. We find it hard to grapple with the real God who allows suffering and evil, but who also enters into our messy world to help us, at great personal cost. As adults we have to allow the real God to stand up: we must accept God as infinite mystery. We ourselves like to be accepted for who we really are: so does God!

It is in the person of Jesus that we meet the real God 'on legs'! But how he goes about things surprises some and shocks others. Amazement is an important word in the Gospels: anger is another – the anger of those who because of vested interests want a different sort of God. We ourselves struggle to allow God to respond to human suffering and evil in a round-about and tortuous way rather than deal with it immediately and decisively. God is indeed mysterious in every way.

Who Could Have Guessed?

Who could have imagined that God would become human, would experience our life in its joy and misery, and would allow himself to experience the depths of human malice in his passion? Why would he die for our sakes in a gigantic effort to reveal his love? Who could have imagined that he would rise from the dead only to come back to us, hold nothing against us, but instead invite us to *'walk in newness of life'* until finally we share eternal joy with him?

Imagine for a moment that the Incarnation has not yet taken place, but that it is promised. There are as yet no Gospels. Now suppose that someone posts on Facebook a story with images showing a young man doing amazing things for the poor, the sick, the insane, the hungry, even for the dead. The news would go viral! Travel sales would rocket as people flock to see and meet this man for themselves. Your own big worry would be, *'Can I get to see him?'* and *'Would he want to see me?'* How would it affect you to know that you have been included, and invited into the companionship of this amazing person; that you are important to him; that your future is secure; that death is not the end of everything for you? Who could have guessed that life could open out like this?

But before you can get to Galilee, fresh news comes in: this good man has been murdered by the religious and political authorities. All is lost; your hopes are dashed, you are back to where you were before. Then another post comes in: *'The story is that he is alive again! Yes, he did die all right, but they have seen him, and they're saying that he has broken through death and is promising endless life with God to all comers, good and bad! Forgiveness and mercy are given to everyone, and there's only one rule from now on: we are to love one another because he loves us all. Yes, this includes enemies!'*

Who could have guessed? We need to read the Good News of God's project for humankind with that kind of excitement, allowing our minds to be blown and our hearts broken open.

Enter Jesus

Before Jesus showed up, the band of young Galilean fisherfolk led by Simon Peter had their own hazy images of God. They would have recalled in the psalms the goodness of God in their past history, but where was that God now? When they pondered the Roman occupation of the Promised Land that was theirs, they must have wondered whether God was punishing them or had forgotten them. God, they felt, was certainly delaying his entry on stage to sort things out.

But once Jesus arrived, things began to move dramatically. Initially there was a roller-coaster of success and wonder-working; this was followed by ghastly failure when Jesus was murdered, and finally – against all the odds – there emerged the joy-filled mystery of his resurrection. The irruption into their lives of God in the person of Jesus turned everything upside-down and inside-out. It offered them meaning to the enduring puzzle of suffering, evil and death, and it convinced them that God was indeed on their side. But not in the ways they had hoped: Jesus did not fit the bill of a political Messiah. He was literally 'something else'. How much they *understood* must have been quite limited: but their belief that something radical had happened was grounded in the solid evidence of Jesus' life, death and resurrection. That is why they wrote the Gospels and did what he had commanded them to do. This present book is grounded in the same solid evidence. Christian faith is not a Santa myth but an adult faith based on reasonable belief. We might have preferred the 'Good News' to have a different shape, but this is what we are given.

Light in the Darkness

The Christian revelation breaks open the mystery of tragedy and sin by revealing God's extraordinary intervention in Jesus Christ. It emerges as total surprise that the divine goal is not simply to be nice to everyone, nor to liberate the Jews from the Romans, but to liberate humankind – and creation itself – from what St Paul calls its '*bondage to decay*' (Romans 8:21). Further, this liberation was to be achieved, not as expected by force, but instead by love, service, forgiveness, and mercy.

Evil is challenged head-on by Jesus. He brings it into sharp relief by revealing its dire consequences but also its dramatic resolution. The divine strategy reconfigures human history: suffering, evil and death are 'put in their place'. Evil is contained, enfolded and transformed. The boundaries of the jigsaw of which we spoke earlier emerge from the dark mist surrounding them, and now, two thousand years on, we find they are still solidly in position!

The Good News

Much writing on the topic of God and evil tends to omit the critical fact of God's *historical intervention in Jesus Christ.* But this reality has pride of place here: without it our discussion would remain on the level of ideas and speculation. God reveals the divine resolution of the problem of suffering and evil to us in concrete fashion and personal form so that anyone, educated or not, can grasp it. This is why the Bible is the all-time best-seller in the history of printing! The life, death and resurrection of Jesus provide the supreme revelation of the goodness of God: speculation about God yields to fact, the fact that God so loves the world as to entrust his Son to us, no matter how we respond. We learn about the real God who does not punish humankind for its wrongdoing but liberates us so that we can live out lives of goodness and reach the happiness for which we long. All of this takes place at God's pace, not ours, so we have to batten down the hatches when life is rough, weather the storms patiently, and play our own role in challenging evil while forgiving those who commit it.

The Hebrews told their stories of God's interventions in their lives. To be Christian is to find oneself in possession of a new and dramatic instalment of the story. The compelling argument for the goodness of God is the mystery of the Cross, which when decoded means '*God loved me and gave himself for me*' (Galatians 2:20). It has been said that if all the Gospels had been destroyed long ago except the single verse, '*God so loved the world that he gave his only Son, so that everyone who believes in him may not perish but may have eternal life*' (John 3:16) – that would be enough.

God has not told us how he managed creation: he invites us to puzzle that out for ourselves. But he *has* told us how he manages our salvation, so we will now explore the divine response to suffering and evil. Here is my simple version of God's project.

LET US SAVE EVERYONE!

Despite the state of the world, the divine Persons have never wavered in their good intentions for the well-being of humankind and of our universe.

Their project is intended to encompass everything, including evil.

Through the emergence of Jesus Christ into our world, their enterprise has taken a decisive and dramatic leap forward.

The divine decision is to sort out the mess we make, not from a safe distance, but from inside human history. Nor do the divine Persons rely on law and punishment to improve human behaviour. Instead, their intervention is personal and is centred on winning people over through love of a special kind.

The decisive action of entering into human history is a costly gift of God to us. God's Son gets caught into the tangled web of human suffering, evil and death. But he breaks free from within; liberated himself, he liberates us so that we can walk in newness of life, and he gives us what we need for sustained development in goodness.

God makes us good, very good (Genesis 1:28). Now God is

working to restore us to our innate goodness, to make us grow in love so that we can live happily with one another and with God. God achieves this by establishing with us a new depth of relationship, so that we become the friends of God and of one another. The friendship of the three divine Persons is the key loving action of God in our world.

Divine friendship brings about in us interior change and conversion, because friendship changes people. Through friendship with Jesus we come to see reality as God sees it (this is faith); we come to love reality as God loves it (this is charity) and we come to collaborate with God in working toward our eternal destiny (this is hope). Interior change is difficult, but slowly we become transformed. People who live out of faith, hope and charity have a special quality about them! We become friends of Christ and take our cues from the Good Spirit rather than from the world around us. We become 'good' in the way that God is good. Spread out in time and space, the community of those who are becoming like God begins to take shape.

The divine project is already in operation, moving forward in some areas, suffering setbacks in others, but always holding a steady course. It advances as silently as biological growth. 'Day and night the seed is growing even if the farmer does not understand how' (see Mark 4:27). It takes God all the time in the world to bring in the harvest. We do not have to understand God's action but to accept and collaborate with it: we are to be carriers of this transformation; thus the community of the friends of God continues to grow.

God is indefatigable and keeps everyone, bad and good, in view. Human malice only calls forth new dimensions in the divine strategy. More love is needed and provided. The persistence of suffering and evil should not dismay us, since it does not dismay God. As

St Thomas Aquinas pointed out, 'For a thing to be good, all the details must conspire properly; for a thing to go wrong, only one defect is needed'. Failure, then, is to be expected, but instead of eliminating it, God works through it to bring good. We see this on Calvary, where the greatest evil yields the greatest good. Sometimes we also see it happening close to hand, as when people develop a greatness of heart that might have passed them by if their hearts had not been stretched by suffering.

Because God is supremely good, God only allows suffering and evil because he can bring good out of them. So until the end of time humankind will continue to experience the consequences of evil. God does not shield us from pain and sorrow but stands with us so that we may grow rather than diminish through them. We become capable of steadily choosing the loving response to situations as they arise. Our unavoidable suffering, patiently endured, is redemptive. This positive attitude to evil works to transform us and thereby transforms the world.

FOR REFLECTION

Notice what attracts you in the above sketch of the divine purposes for humankind. Pray over it, ponder it, discuss it, disagree with it, or simply contemplate it and say 'Wow!' The important thing is to engage with it.

A LETTER TO THE EPHESIANS

Is my version of the divine project based on what I as an optimist would like to believe or is it grounded on something more solid?

While my account is drawn from across the New Testament, the *Letter to the Ephesians* (1:3-23) presents in summary form the magnificence and all-encompassing nature of God's response to the challenge of suffering and evil. This letter was written within fifty years of Jesus' life, by Paul or one of his disciples. Ephesus, the Roman capital of Asia Minor, had become a missionary centre for Christianity. It is good to remember that the Ephesians who got this letter almost two thousand years ago had none of the educational advantages that we have. Many of them could not read, and they would have had between them one single copy of the letter. But they treasured this account of God's saving work in Christ, they lived out of it and shared it, so that it has come down to us today.

The text itself is a great poem celebrating God's project in human history. Call it a love-poem, the story of the three divine Persons who lavish all they have on us, their beloveds.

To catch on to the limitless breadth of vision behind the divine project, think of a great and worthwhile human project like the 1948 United Nations Charter for Human Rights: it in fact embodies many Gospel values, especially that of the dignity of the human person. Imagine the initial vision of that Charter, then the worlds of detailed planning needed for it to become operative for succeeding generations. Add in the human factors that continually beset its progress – misunderstanding, denial and opposition. This gives a backdrop against which to appreciate the depth of planning which lies behind the divine project. If you look back to the section on divine providence you will see why we can rightly hope that God will succeed: we largely fail when attempting something for the good of the world, whereas God includes *everything* in the divine plan.

Note too that the divine project is not a stop-gap remedy for an earlier plan that has gone haywire because of human waywardness. The generous intentions of God in our regard were set before history got going: we were chosen before the foundation of the world for a divine inheritance – life with God – and Christ was to bring us to it. The difference is that now due to our distortion of the divine plan we have to be won back to this inheritance through costly love.

For the moment just enjoy the text below without analysing it too much. Notice phrases that catch your imagination or touch your heart. The deeper you are drawn into the vision presented here, the better you will be able to accommodate suffering and evil. Ask the Holy Spirit to help you to understand what God is trying to get across to you, but if you find the text too condensed, try focusing on the word 'all' which is used nine times here. Let it expand your imagination: in this way you will grapple with the unfettered imagination of God.

WE ARE BLESSED AND CHOSEN
EPHESIANS 1:1-23

Blessed be the God and Father of our Lord Jesus Christ, who has blessed us in Christ with every spiritual blessing in the heavenly places, just as he chose us in Christ before the foundation of the world to be holy and blameless before him in love.

We Have a High Destiny

He destined us for adoption as his children through Jesus Christ, according to the good pleasure of his will, to the praise of his glorious grace that he freely bestowed on us in the Beloved (Jesus).

We are Saved by Christ's Death

In him we have redemption through his blood, the forgiveness of our trespasses, according to the riches of his grace that he lavished on us.

The Divine Project: 'Save all: Lose Nothing!'

> *With all wisdom and insight he has made known to us the mystery of his will, according to his good pleasure that he set forth in Christ, as a plan for the fullness of time, to gather up all things in him, things in heaven and on earth.*

God Will Succeed

> *In Christ we have also obtained an inheritance, having been destined according to the purpose of him who accomplishes all things according to his counsel and will, so that we, who were the first to set our hope on Christ, might live for the praise of his glory.*

The Spirit is Given Us

> *In him you also, when you had heard the word of truth, the gospel of your salvation, and had believed in him, were marked with the seal of the promised Holy Spirit; this is the pledge of our inheritance towards redemption as God's own people, to the praise of his glory. I have heard of your faith in the Lord Jesus and your love towards all the saints, and for this reason I give thanks for you as I remember you in my prayers.*

The Greatness of God's Power

> *I pray that the God of our Lord Jesus Christ, the Father of glory, may give you a spirit of wisdom and revelation as you come to know him, so that, with the eyes of your heart enlightened, you may know what is the hope to which he has called you, what are the riches of his glorious inheritance among the saints, and what is the immeasurable greatness of his power for us who believe, according to the working of his great power.*

> *God put this power to work in Christ when he raised him from the dead and seated him at his right hand in the heavenly places, far above all rule and authority and power and dominion, and above every name that is named, not only in this age but also in the age to come.*

Evil Is Conquered

> *And he has put all things under his feet and has made him the head over all things for the Church, which is his body, the fullness of him who fills all in all.*

FOR REFLECTION

We sketched earlier the dark pages of our lives: now we re-contextualise them in the light of the death and resurrection of Jesus. We spoke also of the importance of a candle on a lonely path in the dead of night. Imagine yourself now inching along your path with a big Paschal Candle, such as is used at Easter to symbolise the light-bearing presence of Christ in a darkened world.

ASSEMBLING THE JIGSAW

Let's now draw out some of the main themes from this remarkable text of *Ephesians*. We are searching for the key pieces of the jigsaw – those that give us the boundary lines or the parameters of God's project. Some pieces are easier to spot than others: think of yourself as being given a code to decipher the code which unlocks the mystery of evil. The key point is to catch on to the fact that sin, suffering, evil and death are no longer untamed destructive forces: they are encompassed by God's project. Human projects, no matter how well-intentioned, can fall down when difficulties arise because left to ourselves we are incapable of sustained development. It is often beyond us to integrate human waywardness into our plans. Hence marriages, benevolent schemes, educational theories, national plans, and efforts to secure sustained peace can frequently fall apart.

Ephesians asserts that God's project is different. By the stretching of divine love to the limit our hard hearts are won over. In Christ God is bent over backwards on the Cross and his love is poured out, to prove to us that we are infinitely loved and called to love. Martin Luther King used to say that only love is big enough to transform enemies into friends: hate can be conquered, but only by love. In *Ephesians* we see the early Church expressing its conviction that divine love is hard at work, that it is already engaging with the dark side of human history and radically transforming it.

You might like to identify some boundaries of the jigsaw of suffering and evil for yourself before reading my list below. I suggested above that the word 'all' offers plenty of material for your insights.

Here are my parameters:

1. The Project is Divine

This is no impersonal computer-generated project! It originates in personal love, the love of the three divine Persons – *God the Father; Jesus*

Christ, and 'the promised Holy Spirit'. They work together on the divine project with joy and love, *'according to their good pleasure'*. Because they freely originate everything, they can achieve their project *'with immeasurable power'*. Since in Christian belief, *'nothing is impossible to God'*, we can have confidence that their project will succeed. The divine dream is not just a future hope: it is already being realised. Christ is central to it and is referred to in our text some twenty times. He fulfils the divine intentions perfectly, and so God's world-transforming project is well under way.

2. The Project is Comprehensive

God's project is for *'the fullness of time'* and it will gather up *'all things'*. So nothing is left out! The plan takes in everything, including failure and evil. It is forward-looking, heading to its goal. Notice the sweep of time involved: *'before the foundation of the world… a plan for the fullness of time… for this age and the age to come'*. The project is also historical, not imaginary or delusional – it moved into action at a certain time: *'when you heard and believed… when the Father raised Jesus from the dead'*. God's final intention for the cosmos is clear: everything will be brought together eventually. God's panoramic vista ensures that evil is being comprehensively dealt with.

3. The Project is Good News for Us All

Great leaders like to plan new world orders, but usually their plans are good for themselves but bad for others: Communism under Stalin involved the elimination of millions of independently-minded people. The divine project is totally different: God intends that every human being should grow to their fullness by being adopted into the divine family. We are all *'chosen and destined'* for this. Nobody is an outsider. God showers on each one of us *'every spiritual blessing'*: God holds nothing back. Nothing is done out of anger or superiority. Jesus is named as the *'Beloved'* and by being linked to him we become beloveds too. Note that the word 'me' – so important to us today! – is not used in the text, because God has in view nothing less than the totality of humankind. This is what grounds the Christian hope that everyone, bad and good, will ultimately be saved. Earth's population is 7.4 billion now; add to this number the billions that went before us and those yet to emerge on earth, and you catch on to the fact that God thinks big!

The 'good news' continues. We are now enabled to be *'holy and blameless'* and to live with God in love. This is our *'inheritance'*. What we yearn for most of all as human persons is to enjoy good and satisfying relationships. This will be given us and we will be satisfied forever. The hope of this great inheritance can keep us going through difficult times. We can dream about it, wonder about it, and look forward to enjoying it to the full. We are already *'rich'* and *'glorious'* as adopted members of the family of God. And no matter what our failings, we are being enabled to reach the fullness of our potential. We will emerge finally 'at our best', which really means that we will become *'like God'*.

4. All Is Forgiven

Human schemes carry sanctions and punishments to ensure compliance. Law-breakers are excluded from society, deprived of freedom, tortured, left to rot in jails, eliminated. But in the divine project there are no losers. Nothing is held against us. The words that haunt us – 'punishment', 'purgatory', hell', 'shame', 'guilt' – do not occur in the text. Instead, *'the forgiveness of our trespasses'* is calmly announced. We don't have to understand why it should be so, but we do have to let the text speak for itself. If evil is a mystery, its resolution is a greater one. Imagine if all the prisons of the world were suddenly emptied, and you get the idea! Bishop Desmond Tutu, quoted already in the Introduction, puts it humorously: *'We may be surprised at the people we find in heaven. God has a soft spot for sinners. His standards are quite low.'* In a famous sermon, 6 Nov 2005, he proclaims: *'God's family has no outsiders. Everyone is an insider. When Jesus said, "I, if I am lifted up, will draw..." Did he say, "I will draw some, and tough luck for the others"? He said, "I, if I be lifted up, will draw all." All! All! All! − Black, white, yellow; rich, poor; clever, not so clever; beautiful, not so beautiful. All! All! It is radical. All! Saddam Hussein, Osama bin Laden, Bush − all! All! ... Gay, lesbian, so-called "straight;" all! All! All are to be held in the incredible embrace of the love that won't let us go'.*

Our freedom is achieved not by our own efforts but through the extravagant generosity of Christ: our redemption is *'through his blood'*. Over the centuries these words have connoted the dark side of the passion. But Christian faith goes beyond this: in Xavier in Northern Spain, a full-sized wooden crucifix was found in the thirteenth century. All the pain of the passion is there, but the face is quietly radiant. The image is called 'The Smiling Christ'. His smile includes serenity and peace but there is more. A smile is a welcoming gesture: it says, *'Come, you are safe here. Have no fear. My heart is open to you. Let us explore and deepen our friendship.'* Jesus' smile reveals his heart and the heart of his Father. All has been transformed by love.

Our Response

We are now *'to live for the praise of God's glory'* which means that we are to acknowledge the goodness and greatness of God as shown in the divine project. On a personal note, I notice that writing this section has given me joy, hope and energy. It has strengthened my conviction − which sometimes gets obscured − that it is profoundly right for me to commit myself to the designs of God. The divine project to save all things is a safety net, no matter how world history lurches along, no matter how badly we disfigure our precious little planet or how our personal history unfolds. If I ask where does my energy, hope and joy come from, it seems not unreasonable to attribute them to God: they are a sign that I am catching on to what God is doing, or better, that God is catching on to me and drawing me more deeply into the divine arrangement of things. In Ignatian terms, this Godward attraction is consolation!

Ephesians offers a marvellous outline of God's dream for our eternal wellbeing. It is within these parameters that the troublesome pieces of our jigsaw can be set. If we don't see how the most jagged ones can be fitted in, God does: *'the immeasurable greatness of his power'* is already being *'put to work'*. The God who *'raised Jesus from the dead'* can cope with the worst we can do. Our task is to trust what is being revealed to us, and to move along with confidence in otherwise forbidding territory, where good and evil, wheat and weeds are allowed to grow together until the harvest (Matthew 13:24-30).

MY LIFE IS GOOD!

Josephine Bakhita was born around 1869 in Darfur in Sudan. At the age of nine, she was kidnapped by slave-traders, beaten till she bled, and bore innumerable scars as a result. In the slave-markets of Sudan she had the humiliation of being sold to five different masters. Finally, in 1882, at the age of thirteen, she was bought by an Italian and brought to Venice.

There she came to know a totally different kind of 'master' – the living God, the God of Jesus Christ. Up to that time she had known only masters who had despised and maltreated her. Now, however, she heard that there is a Master above all masters, the Lord of all lords, and that this Lord is good, goodness in person. She came to know that this Lord also knew her, that he had created her – that she too was loved and awaited by none other than him. What was more, this Master had himself accepted long ago to be flogged for her sake.

Now she had true hope – no longer simply the modest hopes of enduring day by day or finding masters who would be less cruel, but the great hope which she expressed as follows: 'I am definitively loved and no matter what happens to me I am awaited by this love. And so my life is good.'

She became a Religious Sister and spent her life sharing with others the liberation she had experienced through her encounter with the God of Jesus Christ.

FOR REFLECTION

Most of us have difficulty in believing that we are worthwhile. How far do you know in your heart that you are loved and awaited? What was God doing while Bakhita endured the life of a slave? Imagine what Bakhita's prayer was like once she had found God. Does your prayer express gratitude and joy?

WHEN YOUR WORLD FALLS APART

On a Friday in spring, about the year 30 in the Christian era, the hopes of Mary of Nazareth are shattered. Her son, whom she loved beyond measure, has been murdered. How does she react? Colm Tóibín's novel about Mary, *The Testament of Mary*, is written from the perspective of an older disillusioned Mary who is consumed by grief and anger. In Tóibín's version of events, she does not believe that her son's death was worth it and she dismisses the cult that is growing around him. Her world of expectation has fallen apart.

Tóibín's presentation, although imaginative, is wide of the mark and lacks historical foundation. The weight of Christian tradition goes another direction. Out of the drama of Calvary came a new insight into what was going on deep down, and we can make it our own especially when for us things fall apart. The message can be expressed in six words: *'Unavoidable suffering, patiently endured, is redemptive.'*

The Dynamic of the Cross

How does God bring good out of evil? In the Emmaus story (Luke 24:13-35), Jesus makes a remarkable statement which offers in cryptic form his personal perspective on his passion. Speaking to two disciples on the road whom he – perhaps humorously – calls *'foolish and slow of heart'* he says: *'Was it not necessary that the Christ should suffer these things and then enter into his glory?'* (Lk 24:26). He had set himself a goal to achieve: not the goal of suffering, but of revealing to the world the unmeasured and forgiving love of the Father. Now he says that he has achieved that goal, even though it has meant great suffering. In that sense, the Cross, he says, was *'necessary'*.

Here we have the first articulation of the healing dynamic of the Cross and it comes from Jesus himself. It is as if he were to say, *'because of what has emerged from my passion, I am grateful for it, terrible though it was.'*

This is no glorification of suffering, as some Christians have thought. It is rather an insight that by the grace of God, good can emerge from evil. Contemplating this, as Mary of Nazareth did, Christians came to see that *it is in the divinely arranged order of things that goodness will emerge when evil is patiently endured.* In other words, suffering can carry a good energy when we accept it well.

Our eyes can be *'opened'*, as were the eyes of the Emmaus disciples (Luke 24:31), and we can come to see that God allows evil only to bring great good out of it. God respects the free will of human beings and the malice they can perpetrate, but all the time God is working within the evil to transform it into good. Jesus' torturers do their worst. But Jesus endures in patient love, and by raising Jesus from death, the Father confirms that this is the divinely chosen way to deal with evil. It is by his attitude of heart that Jesus outwits evil, sin and death. These destructive forces are encompassed by a totally surprising love; and so against all expectation, they become the occasion of great good.

A New Love Is Born

The dynamic of the Cross shows God's extraordinary capacity to turn a disastrous situation inside out and draw limitless good from it. The Christian insight into suffering is that new meaning – *divine meaning* – is given to what we endure at such a humble level – there is no glory around suffering. But can we prove that God is indeed at work at the heart of our pain? Not indeed in a manner that will satisfy a sceptic. This insight emerges not from rigorous logic or a philosophy of suffering. It comes instead through quiet contemplation of the particular way in which Jesus bore his pain on Calvary. There a new love is born and the inner nature of divine loving is revealed to the world. The power of this love is such that it unfolds in his resurrection. Had he not faced his torments with this love there would be nothing to show from his death. In a deep sense the world *had* fallen apart; only a limitless love could mend it.

The validity of the dynamic of the Cross is to be found on every page of the human journey. The stories scattered across these pages verify it, and each of us can reach this insight for ourselves. Reflect on your own life and notice some occasion when good came from a suffering you endured. You will notice a gleam of resurrection, even if in a minor key. Your present inner equilibrium shows that you have been able to come to terms with unavoidable suffering, and that's a remarkable thing. Why, after all, do you not fall apart when things go wrong for you? We asked earlier in commenting on *Matryona's House* whence comes the extraordinary resilience of people when faced with disasters or daunting challenges? By enduring patiently the vast majority of humankind live out the dynamic of the Cross without adverting to the fact. In small victories over evil and sorrow, a hint of the resurrection is given to the eye that can see.

THE SCARS OF THE YEARS

An example of this unawareness of something good going on deep down in us is given in the novel, *A Whole Life*, by Robert Seethaler. It tells the story of Andreas Egger: little that is remarkable happens in his life when looked at from the outside. But deep down surprising growth is taking place: it is the making of a person.

> *Egger is brought to live in a valley in the Austrian Alps when he is four years old. He has no memory of where he has come from but knows that his mother is dead. He is fostered by a heartless farmer who beats him regularly and breaks a bone in his back so that he becomes known to the local children as 'gammy leg'. He thinks, speaks and walks slowly, but shows a patient wisdom. He adjusts to life as it unfolds and remarks that 'scars are like*

years. One follows another, and it's all of them together that make a person who they are'.

His heart is secretly open to the feminine, and he falls in love with Marie, who also, as it happened, has a scar. He judges that to be worthy of her he needs a steady job, so he joins a construction company in erecting cable cars in the valley, and takes a quiet pride in his exhausting work. They marry and she becomes pregnant, but an avalanche sweeps her and their little house away while he is in the valley, and for years he lives in pure sorrow at her loss.

With the arrival of the Second World War, he volunteers for the Nazi army, but is turned down. In 1942, however, he is called up and sent 'to liberate the East' against Russia. He is soon captured and for eight nameless years endures the horrors of a prisoner-of-war camp. On returning home he becomes a tour guide in his valley, and helps many people. He is kind, but in his off-hand and gruff manner. His style is to accept what comes and avoid doing wrong to anyone who crosses his path.

Life and the work on the mountains take their toll; everything about his body becomes more warped and crooked; his hands begin to fail him. His final years are spent in a lonely hut over-looking the valley. He has nothing, and it is enough. He has had his dreams; some were torn from his hands, others were, he feels, fulfilled. Overall he judges that many things had not gone too badly. He had loved, and cherished an intimation of where love could lead. He hadn't felt compelled to believe in God, though he was nominally a Catholic. He did not pray. 'There's nothing after death, because if there were a god, his heavenly kingdom wouldn't be so far away.' He feels like a remnant from some long-buried time, someone who had survived so many things. He dreams of Marie and says to her, 'There's so much to tell you.

This whole, long life'. Without knowing where he had come from or where he was going, he can look back without regret at the time in-between, 'with laughter and utter amazement'.

FOR REFLECTION

How does this story affect you? Do you feel, perhaps, that it tells a universal theme? Has your life something in common with Egger's unremarkable existence which is yet so rich in mystery?

THE DYNAMIC OF THE CROSS

It may be helpful to tease out that highly-compressed truth which we have called 'the dynamic of the Cross'.

Unavoidable suffering

Jesus takes up a clear attitude in the face of human suffering: he does all he can to remove it: he was no passive spectator of the pain of his times. He went about *'doing good'*. The message is that if suffering can be avoided or remedied, we must act as Jesus did against it. We will say more about this later.

But there is much suffering that cannot be avoided: tragedies; oppression; genocides; the suffering of those we love; the spoiling of the environment; natural catastrophes; partings; sickness; old age and dying.

Patiently endured

Unavoidable suffering has to be endured. But it can be endured in quite opposite ways. We can resent it, blame others for it, deny it, as when people refuse to accept their ageing or their dying. We can curse it, grow hard of heart because of it, become diminished by it. We can refuse to forgive others who wrong us.

Or we can decide to endure unavoidable suffering, not with a stoic mentality, but with patience. Why would we do this? For Christians it is because of faith in the example set by Jesus. Hidden in this patience is love. *'The one who endures to the end will be saved'* (Mark 13:13). Jesus says this, and also lives it. From his prayer in the Garden we see that he wished to avoid his Passion if that were possible. Likewise for us. We struggle to move from negativity and reluctance to quiet acceptance. We may not embrace the pain, though St Paul can speak of the joy he experiences in suffering out of love for his churches (Colossians

91

1:24). Such joy comes from the fact that suffering with another in mind can be the occasion of showing them great love.

Redemptive

We do not say that patient endurance *may be* redemptive: we assert that it is so. The truth of the assertion lies on the bedrock of the resurrection of Jesus Christ. We can say, *'We know from what happened in Jesus' passion that the dynamic of the Cross actually works; it is effective.'* Even if a person has no knowledge of the Christian order of things, their patient endurance is transformative though they know nothing of it. What matters is that each of us should get into the flow of the divine project by taking up a positive attitude to the suffering that we cannot avoid. In this way we become collaborators with God in the resolution of the problem of evil. While Jesus brings about in a radical way the redemption and salvation of humankind, we appropriate it over time. So the dynamic of the Cross is lived out day by day. It is there waiting for us. Jesus invites us to take up our own crosses daily and to follow him – this involves wrestling with ourselves so that we move from enduring things with bad grace to accepting them with good grace. In this way the work of our redemption is steadily carried on.

What do we mean by **redemptive**? 'Redemption' literally means 'being bought back' as when a free person had been sold into slavery and later bought back and set free by a friend. In trying to capture the great mystery set out in *Ephesians*, Christians say that Jesus 'bought us back' or freed us so that we could live holy and good lives in God's presence. An alternative term is *salvation*, which comes from the Latin and means 'health'. Together the two words indicate that we are freed and made whole and healthy in regard to relationships with God, others and ourselves. Other words can help unfold the mystery further: unavoidable suffering, patiently endured is *life-giving, transfor-*

mative, grace-filled. The dynamic of the Cross reveals that God's ways of dealing with evil are strange indeed! God does not only defeat sin but makes use of it in the process. The passion is the supreme indicator of how God uses the worst of human wrong-doing to transform evil. Sin, the supreme obstacle to the emergence of God's kingdom, now plays a pivotal role in its growth.

God shows endless respect for human freedom, yet is able to change the wayward heart from evil to good. We will explore this mysterious process later, but the Gospels stress the fact of it: even as Jesus dies, the evil attached to his death bears good fruit. So the pagan centurion in charge of the execution says in surprise and admiration, '*This was a good man*' (Luke 23:47). Again, '*the crowds who had gathered for this spectacle returned home, beating their breasts*' (v. 48). They had come for entertainment; they went away repentant.

Then came an event which shattered all previous understanding about suffering and evil, death and the after-life.

The Resurrection

It is impossible for us to grasp fully the meaning of the resurrection of Jesus, but the resurrection grasps and transforms everything. The Jesuit theologian Karl Rahner suggests that Jesus' resurrection is like the first eruption of a volcano which shows that God's fire already burns in the innermost depths of the earth. In God's good time everything shall come to glow with that fire.

Resurrection, then, is not Jesus' own private destiny. It is rather a surface indication that all reality has begun to change in the decisive depth of things. Whereas our volcanoes are destructive, the divine 'volcano' pours out upon an unsuspecting world the life-giving love and mercy of God, and makes all things new. What was hopeless and doomed to futility is being transfigured. The desert of human history blooms with a new flower, that of forgiving love.

We often wonder why Jesus did not simply cure all our ills with a sweep of his healing hands. We have to accept in faith that God has chosen a better way. God is keeping pace with us as we make our pilgrim way along. He has redeemed the innermost centre of our earthly existence. There is no longer an abyss between God and creation. God is mysteriously present in everything that is made, no matter how small or humble. He is in each of us. We have become children of the resurrection, and already our lives are being irradiated by a love that *'does not come to an end'* (1 Cor 13:8). Our miseries and fears are the birth-pangs of the new creation, the revelation of the daughters and sons of God. Like Jesus, we suffer, but only to enter into glory (Luke 24:26).

Does God Suffer Too?

Granting that divine suffering is unique and beyond our comprehension, can we say that God knows suffering from within, and is not simply a spectator of a groaning world? Since the Holocaust, the issue of a God suffering in the pain of human beings has come to the fore as never before. We tend to think that God is above all suffering, but is it so? We can say a word about each of the three divine Persons in this regard.

The Son

Through the Incarnation of the Son, suffering enters into the life of God in a personal way. In Jesus one of the divine Persons suffered. The passion of Jesus reveals to us that the nature of God's love is a *suffering* love. Moreover Jesus is the head of the Body of Christ which in principle includes everyone, and suffering defines humankind. But *if one member of the body suffers, all suffer together with it* (1 Corinthians 12:26). This grounds Pascal's statement that Jesus will be in agony until the end of the world because he suffers in his body, which is humankind. Jesus experienced that sense of abandonment which many of us feel when we are visited by heavy suffering. He is with us in our pain. When we are with someone else in pain we experience helplessness; does he feel helpless as he sits with us in our grief? Recall Etty Hillesum's words to God: *'You cannot help us.'* There is a mysterious truth in this statement: God has decided to let warped human freedom take its course. But people who suffer greatly are often very patient. In their own way, whether believers or not, they seem to echo the prayer of Jesus: *'Father, into your hands I commend my spirit'* (Luke 23:46). In the Gospels all Jesus' encounters with ordinary people in their pain are charged with life: likewise he is with us in our anguish, he identifies with us, and brings us strength. This is his freely chosen task, and it involves suffering.

The Father

But what of the Father, who often seems so remote? Does he suffer too? Perhaps we can say this: the New Testament centres on the Father as loving the world so much that he allows his Son − with the Son's full agreement − to enter into our human condition to save it. Loving his Son totally as he does, the Father may be understood to suffer too in the agonies of his Son and of all his adopted daughters and sons.

The Spirit

What of the Holy Spirit? *'God's love has been poured into our hearts by the Holy Spirit that is given to us'* (Romans 5:5). Surely again pure love is vulnerable love, so does the Spirit suffer when we do? St Paul remarks that we should not *grieve* the Holy Spirit (Ephesians 4:30) by hurting one another and refusing to forgive, nor *outrage* the Spirit by wilfully persisting in sin (Hebrews 10:29). But grief and outrage bring suffering.

We can spend worthwhile time talking with the three divine Persons about their suffering. It can bring us comfort and strength in our own sorrow and make us more patient with the slow progress of grace in dealing with evil.

GOD IN THE DARK

A friend of mine, Jennie, wrote me the following:

> *About 11 years ago I began to study as a mature student, but I was an angry one. My anger was because of my perceived absence of God in the suffering of people I loved. I hoped that my study might resolve my problem. But as I was about to write a thesis of which the title was 'Suffering in Job', cancer attacked me. Thus, as it turned out, the last essay I wrote was on Jesus' prayer in Gethsemane: 'Father, if you are willing, remove this cup from me; yet, not my will but yours be done'. God's interventions are indeed strange and not without humour sometimes!*
>
> *I struggled before consenting to surgery. The night before the operation was possibly the worst experience of my life. I was alone and terrified. There was the operation ahead, the possibility that I might not come out the other side of it, and there was no escape. Then suddenly I was in Gethsemane and there was a Presence, a very powerful Presence, beside me, which lifted and supported me firmly and gently. It was not a cosy Presence, but one that sustained me and gave me courage and assurance that no matter what the outcome, all would be well. That Presence was still with me when I came to after the operation.*
>
> *The experience of it remains with me, and I now know that God is with us always but particularly in the dark moments when there is nothing else.*

So, you see, I had the answer to my furious questions – not through reading, listening, studying and writing, but through a personal experience which I would never have chosen, and indeed never expected.

FOR REFLECTION

God likes to visit us! '*I stand at the door and knock…*' (Revelation 3:20). But does God visit people like Jennie, and not you? Is it perhaps a matter of our having to endure emptiness and silence, before we can notice that something good is going on? In a pitch dark room, we can be aware if someone is present.

The sense of 'Presence' which Jennie had was delicate, subtle, yet immensely real. This – presumably – is why she typed a capital 'P' for it. It was not cosy but sustaining: it gave her the assurance that no matter whether she lived or died, 'all would be well'. Can you verify this experience of 'Presence' from any of the dark moments of your life? If so, have you found that your earlier images of God have had to change?

DELIVER US FROM EVIL!

God's View of Evil

God sees things not through a narrow peep-hole as I do, but from a comprehensive vantage point, as we suggested above in talking about divine providence. The divine intention works in the present moment, but is massively future-oriented: its long-range goal is to bring eternal joy to everyone. This life is an extended training session for something yet to come. Our life experience can be seen as a matter of being 'got ready' for a quality of life that we can only dimly imagine.

God does not intervene to deliver us from evil at the times and in the ways we wish, but this does not mean that God tolerates evil in a casual way. Instead of eliminating evil and evildoers, God is at work massively with evil, to transform it. The Bible is the history of that struggle. God respects the dynamics of our world in which physical and moral evil are part and parcel of life, but works on a higher level to bring it under control. God works to transform evil into good. In the various incidents related in this book, we find that good emerges from evil in the most surprising ways.

Deliver Us From Evil

Why then does Jesus tell us to ask the Father in the Lord's Prayer to '*deliver us from evil?*' The most startling novelty of the Gospels is the revelation that God **intends to save the bad** as well as the good, and we dare not presume that we are in the camp of the good! We are asking God to deliver us from the evil we are responsible for, so that we may not be lost. The writers of the Old Testament, as we have seen, would have eliminated their enemies. But divine loving draws Jesus in the opposite direction. He takes away the sins *of the world* (John 1:29) and promises that when he is lifted up on the Cross, he will draw *everyone* to himself (John 11:32). He prays for his enemies: '*Abba, forgive* *them for they do not know what they are doing*' (Luke 23:34). This verse was omitted from a number of early manuscripts apparently because it was too much for the copyists to take! And the turbulent history of Christianity shows that Jesus' intention is still too much for many of his people to subscribe to, as shown, for example, in the Crusades and the religious wars following the Reformation.

Evil in the Passion

The term 'Deliver us from evil' is not a naïve request that God may save us from the suffering that evil causes, but a statement of belief that while evil is largely outside our control, it is not outside God's; God can bring us through the evils that we ourselves and others cause. As St John Paul II says, *'There are divine limits to evil'*. In his passion Jesus was not 'delivered from evil' but he was brought through it: evil triumphed in him only for a short time: then came the Resurrection and his full liberation from evil in all its forms. So it will be for us. Jesus turns evil into good by his attitude of patient love. Christians came to call this turn-around of evil the dynamic of the Cross.

We have looked already at the intentions of the various actors in the Passion. What his accusers intend is to do away with Jesus. What Pilate intends is to avoid a riot. What the Roman cohort intends is to dispatch Jesus efficiently. What Mary and the other women intend is to support Jesus in some humble way. What the disciples intend is to save themselves, so they run away. What Jesus intends is to do what he believes the Father is asking of him. But the overarching intention which engages all the others is that of the Father. What the Father intends is to reveal the infinite love of God for the world, especially at the point when humankind is acting at its worst. By revealing so dramatically this great love, the Father hopes to win us over. Hence the title of Von Balthasar's book: *Love Alone: the Way of Revelation*. In the Passion we are to keep our eye on the love revealed there by Jesus for us, which delivers us from the evils of sin and eternal death.

Evil as the Occasion of Good

While we do not understand well what God is about, have we enough evidence to say that while the killing of the Son of God was the worst of evils, it was the *occasion of the greatest good*. Evil, as it were, became unintentionally the *occasion* of the saving of the world. Extravagant forgiveness is visually revealed on the Cross: it then becomes the headline for us to follow. We are to become mediators of reconciliation in a fractured world, and so reverse the downward spiral of evil and hatred.

God's Ways Are Not Ours

Certainly God's ways are not ours. We would resort to the solution of the Great Flood, or at least selective flooding which would eliminate evil people – those 'others' who are 'not like us'! But God goes at the problem differently: God has in view a Final All-inclusive Community of Love. Three elements block the achieving of this Community: sin, suffering and death. While respecting our free will and the slow process of history, God steadily works to unravel the mess we create.

- Sin: Sin is integrated rather than brushed aside because it can become the occasion of good;
- Suffering: Those who suffer can grow in love through their endurance and every step forward on the path of loving helps the world;
- Death: Death is overcome through the resurrection of Christ – he is the first-fruits of the harvest: the rest will follow (1 Corinthians 15:20).

This all seems very cumbersome and uncertain to us, but God judges that all this complexity is worthwhile. Could God do better? The framework of the divine response to suffering and evil is in place.

Enough clues are given us to accept it, but these are not simply on the intellectual level. It is through encounter with the living Jesus, especially in his Passion, that we come to appropriate God's solution, which takes the painful option of transforming evil from within rather than from without. God is not a cosmetic but a heart surgeon!

God tackles evil and suffering at their roots, rather than eliminating them on the surface. We must be patient until the resurrection of the dead reveals a transfigured planet and its all-inclusive community from the inside. Only then will we see that God has answered our prayer, 'Deliver us from evil'.

The Monk's Robe

On the dedication page I quoted the Buddhist Ryokan: '*O, that my monk's robe were wide enough to gather up the suffering people of this floating world*'. God's overarching intention is to gather up the suffering people of this floating world. Strangely, one of the great unseen bonds even between enemies is the shared experience of suffering. Nationalists and Unionists in Northern Ireland discovered this when sharing the same prisons. Solzhenitsyn's *Cancer Ward* illustrates the same truth. God is busy on all fronts!

Like the monk with his robe, we can gather up the suffering which this planet knows so well and present it to God for transforming. This is a mode of creating community. It is a simple form of prayer; the raw material is all around us. I like to pray at my window in the early morning: across from me is an Eye and Ear Hospital. Someone there may feel desolate and unremembered, so trusting in the unforced rhythms of grace I pray that they may be strengthened. Those who pray consistently note that they are drawn beyond particular concerns for their own needs and those of others close to them. They learn to carry the world's pain. In this unexpected way suffering and evil can bring the world very close to God.

ENJOY THIS CRAZY WORLD!

Clodagh Cogley is an Irish survivor of the collapse of a balcony in Berkeley California in June 2015. Six of her student friends died and seven were seriously injured. She wrote on Facebook: 'Hey friends, just an update to let you know how I'm getting on. The fall from the balcony left me with two collapsed lungs, a broken shoulder, a broken knee, five broken ribs and a broken spinal cord... Meaning the chances of me using my legs again are pretty bleak. Not the best odds but I'm moving to a great rehabilitation centre here in San Francisco for two months – it even has dog therapy! – and I intend to give it everything I've got. Who knows, maybe legs have been holding me back all these years and I'll realise my talent for wheelchair basketball. The thing I'm taking from this tragedy is that life is short and I intend to honour those who died by living the happiest and most fulfilling life possible. Enjoy a good dance and the feeling of grass beneath your feet like it's the last time, because in this crazy world you never know when that might be.'

FOR REFLECTION

God doesn't sort things out by rewinding Clodagh's life back to the moment before the tragedy. But does her response show you that God may be at work from the inside and that in a strange way she is being delivered from evil? Does she reveal the capacity of the human spirit somehow to rise to a higher level and to integrate disaster into a new way of life? Could Clodagh, Matryona and Etty have a good conversation together?

PART FOUR:
HOW GOD WORKS IN OUR LIVES

THE HUMAN HEART

I suggested above that God is a cardiac rather than a cosmetic surgeon. Let us explore this. In scripture, the word *heart* is rich in meaning. The heart is the place where I form my attitudes and intentions, where I make my decisive choices. The heart is my conscience, the place where I meet my God. While my heart is mine, it is also God's, since God made it, and God is able to work on it at a depth that is often hidden from me.

The wickedness of the human heart is also a major theme throughout scripture. Jeremiah says, *'The heart is devious above all else; it is perverse – who can understand it?'* (17:9). Jesus speaks of the evil that flows from the heart. *'It is from within, from the human heart, that evil intentions come'* (Mark 7:21). Evil originates in the heart.

But there is hope: God knows the human heart from within, and promises to heal it. *'A new heart I will give you, and a new spirit I will put within you; and I will remove from your body the heart of stone and give you a heart of flesh'* (Ezekiel 36.26). God will transform our hearts and make them good. The strategy of God is to deal with evil by 'heart surgery' – God works to remove what is diseased, and to heal what is wounded, so that there grows within us *'a pure heart'* (Psalm 51). This is God's characteristic work in us; we cannot do it of ourselves. This is what *conversion* means in the Gospels: a re-orientation of the desires in my heart away from what is unhelpful to what is true and good.

Divine Heart Surgery

The focus of God as surgeon is heart *enlargement*! God wants to make our hearts more loving. This occurs slowly and respects the processes of human growth. But can we draw from our experience hints of how God works on us from different angles to bring us into harmony with the dynamic of unrestricted loving which is needed in our world? Some examples follow.

Hard-pressed Parents

In *Far From The Tree*, Andrew Solomon traces the dynamics that operate in parents who are shocked when their child turns out to be very different from their expectations. On the basis of wide research he states that when most such parents look back they see how their 'different' child has enriched them in ways they would never have conceived, ways that are incalculably precious. He found them grateful for the experience which beforehand they would have done anything to avoid. He quotes Rumi, the Sufi poet, who says that the light enters *'at the bandaged place'*. One woman wrote, 'We learn so much from our children – patience, humility, gratitude for other blessings we had accepted before as a matter of course; we learn so much in tolerance, so much in faith; so much in compassion for others; and yes, even so much in wisdom about the eternal values in life'. This is God working on the heart in demanding situations.

DEAD PERFECT?

When I was young I used to long for a time when no-one would be annoying me. Family life did not provide such bliss, but I hoped that when I joined the Jesuits, everyone would be 'at their best'. But it wasn't to be. Year after year, no matter who came and went, there was always someone – if not indeed several – whose style irritated me. Quite simply they weren't up to my high standards, and so I had few real friends. Driven by a perfectionist mode of religious formation, I ended up by making others feel bad about themselves and of course I also felt bad about myself. With the unhappy gift of being able to spot the flaws of others, I was led into what the psychoanalyst Eric Erickson calls 'the life of a thousand little disgusts'. But I knew that to go this way was to fall into a bottomless pit, because people will always be flawed. So where to turn? Become a hermit? Avoid the most irritating brethren? Radiate an aura of dissatisfaction and superiority?

My wake-up moment came out of the blue. In the middle of a psychotherapy session I recounted a dream about my mother lying on a bier: she looked perfect: but she was dead. The therapist stopped me at that point: 'Dead? Perfect?' He closed the session there and then, though he charged me for the full session, which irritated me! Driving home, I suddenly saw the point and burst out laughing. 'It's all been a great mistake!' I said to myself. 'I've put in fifty years trying to be perfect, and I've been killing myself and others in the process. Perfectionism and death go hand-in-hand! But I don't have to live like this!'

I had been busy trying to hold together a world in which my preferences *were central: others had to adjust to them. Driving illustrates what was going on in every area of my life: people overtaking me were driving too fast; people holding me up were driving too slowly! My style of doing things had to be the norm. Now a world of well-intentioned but misguided striving began to dissolve. This was one of the great moments of liberation in my life. Since then I have grown in the belief that I am loved as I am, in my own enduring inadequacy, and that the challenge is not to become 'perfect' but simply to love others in their inadequacy. Their irritating qualities become more manageable when I focus on the mystery of God's love that surrounds them.*

What Do I See?

I view the above experience as an instance of divine heart surgery. I have come to see that my only hope is to begin to look at others and myself from God's point of view. What do I see? Pope Francis puts it succinctly: '*When everything is said and done, we are infinitely loved*'. So I start my morning prayer right there: I ask God to help me believe that I am infinitely loved. When something of that truth has filtered through to my slowly-awakening heart, I ask to accept that my dreadful neighbour is likewise infinitely loved. Try this and you won't be short of material for prayer!

This prayer has a contemplative quality. Contemplation is a high-sounding word, but it means very simply '*taking a long loving look at the real*'. By the 'real' I mean things in their truth, both bad and good. The more I know the reality of myself, the more amazed I am that I should be the focus of God's limitless love. As this comes to dominate my imagination, there is less space for indulging my negativity about others. I become too busy thinking about the unmerited love in which I am wrapped to be getting upset about my 'enemies'. I am more taken up with the Lord's affairs that are going on in my own heart. As I come to love inadequate, flawed, miserable me – use whatever terms you like – I come to love the inadequate, flawed, miserable other who also is not measuring up. Aware then that I am treated with great mercy I become a little more merciful to those around me.

Contemplative Sisters live in constant contact with one another; they can't escape from their enclosure. One of them said to me recently: '*When I'm getting mad with someone, I stop and say in imagination, "What is it like to be you?" This shifts my focus from the irritating quality of the person to the mystery they carry. And since I'll never get to answer my question fully, I can return to it again and again when need arises*'. Not bad at all!

This may seem small stuff, but within it God is doing heart work with a sort of key-hole surgery. And it goes on whenever I encounter insensitive or awkward people. Slowly I am learning not just to tolerate my crabby neighbours but to love them in their crabbiness. I try to believe that this is how they respond to my own crabbiness. Community grows according as I allow the other to be other, unique, different from me, not fitting in to my home-grown expectations. Everyone becomes a divine surprise, and it is my task to move over and make space for them. It's as if God were saying, 'Look whom I brought you!' But that means the enlargement of my small heart, which is God's radical work in me. The war is within, as the poet Hopkins notes, and the skirmishes take place day by day. We have seen how Etty Hillesum makes the same point, when she says that each of us must turn inward and destroy in ourselves all that we think we ought to destroy in others.

FOR REFLECTION

Are you known as someone who can allow other people to be 'other'? Or do you whittle people down to size? How far has God got with your heart surgery?

ME? LOVED AND LOVABLE?!

Margaret, a wife and mother, told me the following story some time back:

> *'I've been going through some sort of mid-life crisis for the past while, wondering where I was heading and what meaning there was in my life and marriage. I've always struggled with the feeling that I'm not good enough, not lovable. At home goodness was measured by performance, so as a child I was always anxious about how I was doing. I became edgy in my relationships and critical of others; but deeper down I was critical of myself. I'd catch myself sometimes saying, 'You're not much good!' Prayer, confession, a course in spirituality, counselling – I tried them all but was still stuck. Then one evening recently I made a mess of things yet again and left someone hurt and raw because I felt I wasn't being properly respected. I was sitting exhausted in my room and began to pray what I can only call 'the prayer of the helpless'.*
>
> *After a while something delicate happened me. It was like the tide coming in quietly on a sandy sunlit beach, slowly covering the sand and rocks. I became aware that I was loved – simply, immensely – and that this love had always been there for me, and always would be. It seemed as if a veil were being drawn over my past unhappinesses; that everything was embraced by love. I was being told, "You are loved and lovable; you need have no fear. You are good." I felt 'forgiven' not in relation to any particular sin, but in relation to my error in not believing this truth – that I am always loved. I heard once in a homily that original sin might be thought of as basic blindness, and that fits me. If you're blind you're missing what is in front of your eyes. I feel my cataracts have been removed and that I'm now in the recovery room.'*

Signs of Change

We tend to think that such experiences are for the chosen few, but perhaps they are intended for us all. They reveal how God goes about transforming the human heart. The love we need to become our best selves is always there, beaming on us: the issue is whether and when we will drop our defences and let it flood in. That can take a lifetime and more in some cases. Why the needed insight or experience is delayed so long is a mystery – I would think that God should 'zap' us earlier on, get through to us and so make life more enjoyable for everyone. But that is another complaint for God from one of his creatures!

Margaret is beginning to see herself in a new way – the way that God sees her. She is coming to see other things from God's perspective too. This is the *'new creation'* that St Paul talks about (Galatians 6:15): it occurs when a person catches on to how lovingly God gazes on them and delights in them. In the light of this inner treasure everything is reconfigured. A new and better story replaces the old tapes about not being 'good enough'. This is the beginning of the *'life in abundance'* which Jesus came to bring (John 10:10). But it takes time for us to believe fully that we are *'the beloved of God'* (see Romans 1:7)! We adapt slowly, and this is not too surprising, since a sea-change is under way. We have to grapple with the imagination of God, whose dreams for us are several sizes too big! God, we have said, is always aiming at the enlargement of the human heart.

Waking Up To Others

In this process of 'waking up' gradually the old world fades and the contours of the new emerge. It will take Margaret the rest of her life to inhabit fully the grace she has been given. She will still have to control well-established habits of criticism and negative judgements of herself and others. But now that she is aware of being limitlessly loved, she is beginning to love others in the same way, because this love within her is for sharing, not for hoarding. Others are no longer rivals or enemies but fellow-patients; like her they are sick but in recovery, all of them members of the one body of Christ. Because she is growing more secure about being loved and wanted, she becomes less demanding of the love of others: the gaping void that is in the human heart is being filled by the Creator's love. Her previous ache to be loved enough by others is yielding to the conviction that God's unwarranted love for her is enough to carry her through. From being focussed on her own need for love, her concern now is to love others in their need. With her new self-awareness she can help them rather than envy them or cut them down to size. She is being invited to endless compassion for those who have not yet arrived where she is at.

Pitied and Chosen

In one of the most dramatic encounters in the Gospels, the extravagance and simplicity of Jesus' love wipes away the darkness of Peter's failures. It is another heart to heart affair. Peter surely had despaired of ever seeing Jesus again, having disowned him three times. But here is Jesus back again, using a great catch of fish to help Peter realise that he is forgiven. The lakeside dialogue is down to essentials – ten words to cover a lifetime. *'Do you love me?' 'Yes.' 'Feed my lambs and sheep!'* Jesus is effectively saying, *'Forget your failures. You've caught on to the fact that I love you. You're a happy man. Now let's go!'* Pope Francis' motto – 'Pitied and Chosen' – catches up this liberating quality: his emphasis on mercy and his own radiant compassion was born when he came to see that his earlier style, however well-intentioned, had been a source of division and hurt. Once liberated from his shame he became free to share his best gifts with the world. The conversion of the heart goes on endlessly.

ONE REGRET

Margaret had one regret. 'What about so many wasted years?' she said. She had to learn to entrust to God the failures of the past, to leave it to God to undo whatever damage she had caused. This made her think of her parents, now dead, who had unintentionally got her off to a bad start. One day she felt free enough to imagine them as present with God to her, and the four celebrated a simple ritual of forgiveness.

When our lives have started badly we can bring much unhappiness on ourselves and others. But God is watching out for opportune moments and gets working on our hearts to set up healthy relationships which cause us to query our destructive ways of proceeding. Even our experience of desolation can help to get us to change tack and move to something better. St Augustine speaks of the restlessness of the human heart which can only be healed when we become aware of God's immense love and respond to it.

FOR REFLECTION

Have you some awareness of the ways in which God keeps softening your heart? Have you ever noticed 'something delicate' happening to you, out of which you have come to own the fact that you are deeply loved? Can you think of persons who helped, and thank them?

TEAMING UP WITH GOD AGAINST EVIL

The New Testament, as we have seen, offers the divine response to suffering, evil and death. But God needs our help to bring that response to bear on everyday life. How do we do this?

Wrestling with God

It is right to ask God's help regarding the various problems that occupy our lives. Often we can do no more than to ask God to take over. But genuine prayer will sometimes take the form of a wrestling with God, when we ask, *'What do you want me to do about this problem?'* Prayer is more than an armchair occupation: God may be looking around for help to address a problem – homelessness, for example – and may be nudging your heart to step into action. If Mary of Nazareth had simply prayed that God would find someone to bring his Son into the world, the Christian story as we know it would not have got under-way. But perhaps the angel visits us too, over and over, looking for our personal response to what God wants to get done!

What, Me?

When we pray, *'Here I am. Send me!'* we emerge from prayer ready to labour with God to bring good out of the bad that is around us. Jesus took this path. Rather than staying in the desert, or becoming a scholar who would offer a philosophy of sin, evil and death, he immersed himself in human affairs and faced down the causes of our pain. He trusted limitlessly in his Father and so must we. Life may continue as painful as before and we may seem to be on the losing side in the battle. Our successes will at best be small ones. But by shaping our lives in light of the dynamic of the Cross, we can glimpse how good can emerge from evil, and this gives us hope that *all* evil and suffering may ultimately be graced. From our experience we can see that compassion, forgiveness and greatness of soul are occasioned by suffering: our hearts are broken open. God works in human betrayal and pain to make us grow in love. God's love is costly, but also tough and enduring: ours must become the same. An engaged Christian life is not for wimps!

Jesus makes himself entirely vulnerable, and this is exploited mercilessly by his enemies in the Passion. The crowds met him on his *Via dolorosa*, his way of sorrows; now he meets us on ours. He expects to find us on our path and on the move. He is looking out for us to strengthen us.

Protesting Against Suffering

We have looked at the dynamic of the Cross which says that *unavoidable suffering, patiently endured, is redemptive.* But since much of the world's suffering is avoidable, Christians can work in innumerable ways to alleviate pain, to rid the world of disease, to help people to die with dignity. Christians are also to be committed to the removal of structural suffering caused by oppressive institutions and systems. The Christian stance is not passivity. Christians are meant to oppose all forms of domination, just as Jesus did. They may themselves suffer or die in the process, as he did. Recall the Christians in El Salvador who drew strength from their companions who had died before them. Jesus was *spent* at the end of his life: we too are to be spent for others, as Matryona was in Solzhenitsyn's story, or as was the widow admired by Jesus: she had put all she had into the Temple treasury – two small copper coins (Luke 21:2). We are to be like Eucharistic bread: taken, blessed, broken, given, consumed. Thus we bring life to the world.

We are to be active in helping others to become free, so far as can be done, so that they may reach their full potential. We are to engage with evil while being patient and forgiving to wrongdoers. Forgiveness is uniquely emphasised in Christianity: God radically forgives us, and we are in turn to forgive others *'from the heart.'* Hatred must have no place in our hearts: instead we are to pray for malicious people. We can love them by thanking God for whatever good is in them and asking that God may break through to them and give them hearts of flesh. God is loving them, watching out for them, working to bring them round, and so we can do the same.

The Mind of an Evildoer

It is not easy to wish good to evildoers and enemies of humanity. But understanding them, so far as can be done, is a help. Recent studies on the evolution of the human brain can soften the revulsion we feel in regard to them, and enable us in imagination to ask them the question posed earlier, *'What is it like to be you?'*

It appears that the human brain has grown in slow stages, with each stage building on the previous one. The first level was the reptilian. Reptiles are cold-blooded creatures. They defend themselves, hunt for food, and reproduce. We share something of this reptilian brain. But reptiles do not look after or defend their young: baby turtles and snakes have to fend for themselves without parental help.

The next dimension to develop was that of creatures which added to their reptilian functions the capacity to look after their young. Here we have the beginnings of relationship between parents and offspring: birds, bees and horses respond to the needs of their young; they nurture them, defend them, equip them to fend for themselves. Relationship, affectivity and emotion – even if primitive – characterise this dimension. It is called the limbic level, because it is proper to warm-blooded creatures with limbs. Again we possess something of this limbic brain.

In humans a third level integrates the other two. It is the neo-cortex (Google it for details of its many layers!). The rational dimension emerges, with its capacity to use elanguage, plan, make decisions, and distinguish right from wrong.

Something Missing

With this framework we can explore a little the inner consciousness of the evildoer. Statistically in a population there will emerge a number of humans who are strong both on the reptilian and the rational level but weak on the limbic level. Due to inherited flaws, bad parenting and unhelpful social influences they have little or no capacity for relating. So they live in an emotionally under-developed state: sympathy and fellow-feeling are undeveloped. Then the primitive self-centred needs of the reptilian interact with the rational capacity of the human, but without the buffer provided by the limbic level, and the result can be monstrous. Such people seem to have no feeling for their victims: hatred eclipses compassion. The evil that follows is not a mistake or oversight: it is calculated, and is in the most literal sense cold-blooded and heartless. Part of the brain of such evil-doers is underdeveloped, and the conscience may be very primitive.

While the objective evil done by such people is clear, what of their subjective guilt? How far are they 'responsible' for what they supposedly do in freedom? How can we judge? We have already looked at the attitudes of suicide bombers. We may need to imprison such people or even kill them in self-defence; but we cannot write them off as having no part in the human race and with no hope of salvation. Often of course we are no match for such people, and indeed their evil qualities seem to fascinate 'good' people. Hitler and Stalin were not short of support from ordinary people like ourselves in carrying out their murderous strategies.

This reinforces the argument that the dividing line between good and evil runs through every human heart: we cannot say naively that we are the 'good people' and over there are the 'bad people'. In the Final Judgement scene in Matthew 25, those focused on for eternal punishment are not gross sinners, not 'bad people': the spotlight is on those *who had done nothing to help their needy neighbour*! The word 'sin' is not mentioned, but the term 'accursed' is used.

While this passage is not to be taken literally as a preview of the end-situation, it is a dramatic call to abandon comfortable passivity and to help those in need.

Solidarity in Suffering

Suffering has a social dimension, and because of the dynamic of the Cross it helps the world. Since we are one body, what happens in one cell affects all the others whether or not we are aware of this.

We have noted that suffering can be relational: shared pain can open the doors between hearts. If we love deeply we are glad to focus our suffering toward the good of others. The humble *Morning Offering* catches up this dynamic, and is an image of Jesus' attitude. The smiling crucifixes at Xavier in Spain and elsewhere silently affirm that for Jesus in his agony the costly love involved was worth it. Quite simply, at the deepest level he died the way he wanted, spending his love for the good of others.

In the Old Testament there is sketched a mysterious figure termed 'the Suffering Servant.' Here we are given a hint that *one person* can bring help and salvation to many by an attitude of patient endurance. We are told that this attitude is highly acceptable to God. *'The righteous one, my servant, shall make many righteous, and he shall bear their iniquities'* (Isaiah 53:11-12). The solidarity of the human race around suffering, evil and its resolution is affirmed. We tend to think that each of us suffers for ourselves and that our pain carries no benefit to others. But it is otherwise in divine thinking.

This throws some light on the patience which enormous numbers of sick and suffering people show, whether they are 'religious' or not. In a crowded A&E Department I am always amazed at the quiet endurance of the patients. They are mostly gracious. Where does that grace come from? Some mysterious force for good is at work even in pain, illness and dying. Surprisingly, the following reflection from the contemplative tradition invites us to look no further than ourselves for its source:

> 'What each one is interiorly,
> face to face with God,
> unknown to anyone,
> is of vital consequence to all.
> And every act of love,
> every act of faith and adoration,
> every mute uplifting of the heart,
> raises the whole world nearer to God.
> From everyone who is in union with God
> there breathes a spiritual vitality, light, strength and joy,
> which reach from end to end of the universe;
> a source of grace to those least conscious of it,
> even to those least worthy of it,
> and knowing nothing of how and whence it comes.'

The 'mute uplifting of the heart' is transformative. It curtails the reality of evil by enveloping it in love. A real change occurs in the world when we are in touch with God.

So *we* have a big role to play in helping to sort out the problem of evil. People do evil things basically because they know little of love. From the divine viewpoint, enveloping them in love is the only way to win them over. Newman speaks of the great mystery which we all carry, but do not know how to share. There is so much goodness locked in people's hearts. If the 2.4 billion Christians in the world, together with all people of goodwill in other religious traditions – and none – shared their inner riches, our world would be transformed!

MEETING LIKE HAPPY THIEVES

In 1996 seven Trappist monks living in the Atlas mountains in Algeria were abducted and murdered by Islamic extremists. Their compelling story was made into the film *Of Gods and Men*. All the monks were Frenchmen who had stayed on, out of solidarity with their Muslim neighbours, despite the death threats issued to foreigners.

Two years beforehand, the prior, Christian de Cherge, wrote a remarkable letter to his friends which he left with his mother in France. He gives his reasons for his willingness to accept what might be in store for him. In the excerpts below we can see how love prevailed in a dreadful situation. More than a last testament, it is a letter of thanks.

> *If it should happen one day – and it could be today – that I become a victim of the terrorism which now seems ready to encompass all the foreigners living in Algeria, I would like my community, my Church, my family, to remember that my life was given to God and to this country.*
>
> *I ask them to be able to associate such a death with the many other deaths that were just as violent, but forgotten through indifference and anonymity.*
>
> *My life has no more value than any other. Nor any less value. In any case, it has not the innocence of childhood. I have lived long enough to know that I share in the evil which seems, alas, to prevail in the world, even in that which would strike me blindly. I should like, when the time comes, to have a clear space which would allow me to beg forgiveness of God and of all my fellow human beings, and at the same time to forgive with all my heart the one who would strike me down.*
>
> *I could not desire such a death. It seems to me important to state this. I do not see, in fact, how I could rejoice if this people I*

love were to be accused indiscriminately of my murder. I know the scorn with which Algerians as a whole can be regarded. I know also the caricature of Islam which a certain kind of Islamism encourages. For me, Algeria and Islam are something different; they are a body and a soul.

(In death) if God wills, I shall immerse my gaze in that of the Father, to contemplate with him his children of Islam just as he sees them, all shining with the glory of Christ, the fruit of his Passion, filled with the Gift of the Spirit, whose secret joy will always be to establish communion and to refashion the likeness, delighting in the differences.

In this "thank you," which is said for everything in my life from now on, I certainly include you, friends of yesterday and today, and you my friends of this place, along with my mother and father, my brothers and sisters and their families.

And you also, the friend of my final moment, who would not be aware of what you were doing: yes, for you also I wish this 'thank you' – and this 'adieu' – to commend you to the God whose face I see in yours.

And may we find each other, happy "good thieves," in Paradise, if it pleases God, the Father of us both.

Amen.

FOR REFLECTION

What gave the prior courage to bear the cost of being a peacemaker? Did he sense that in accepting the dynamic of the Cross, his patient endurance would somehow bring good to those he loved?

Are you willing to be nudged by God to take action that will help someone in need?

FORGIVING FROM THE HEART

'Love your enemies!' This is the most shocking command of Jesus. God forgives all 'enemies' and tries to win them over by love. This is God's fundamental response to evil, and it is to be ours too. If evil is like poison gas, forgiveness draws off its poison and enables the world to breathe freely. But when we experience ourselves as innocent victims of another's evil, forgiveness can seem too much to demand of our poor hearts. Yet if I do not at least try to forgive those who hurt me, I block the flow of the forgiving love of God to them in their need and I remain trapped by the evil they have done me. In this way I obstruct the divine resolution of the problem of evil. This is indeed a strange and unwanted power to have! So it is good to be reminded – over and over until we get the point – that in being forgiven by God for all our personal wrongdoing, we are commissioned to move out to share God's mercy with our own 'enemies.'

For myself, the process becomes easier if I am reminded that I depend utterly on God's forgiveness. When I feel 'righteous' and 'justified' in closing my heart to another who has wronged me, I need to allow the Gospel's cryptic texts to jolt me back to my own shortfalls in the world of relationships. *'Go and do likewise!' 'Wash the feet of others' 'Do not condemn' 'Be compassionate as God is' 'Love others with the limitless love that I have for you.'* The fact that I do not measure up to these commands ushers in a little humility and deflates my feelings of superiority. Awareness that I am always being forgiven by God can break down the wall that some unhappy incident has created between my neighbour and myself. The struggle to forgive breaks the human heart open: grace flows. The evil was real but is being drained of its poison. Things may never be quite the same again between us, but some real good emerges from what was bad. I may not be able to forgive the other fully, but I may be able to walk away from what was done and not allow its pain to shape my future.

God breaks our hearts open by calling us to unrestricted forgiveness. Evil will be resolved and the kingdom of God will be complete when mutual forgiveness presides universally. The New Testament does not delay over the psychological wrestling that forgiveness necessarily involves, but we need to do so. Marina Cantacuzino's recent book, *The Forgiveness Project: Stories for a Vengeful Age* indicates the broad range of meanings which the term 'forgiveness' connotes. Some forty survivors tell the story of their ongoing struggles to forgive. Each story is unique, because the work of forgiveness is intensely personal. I need to repect my own painful efforts on the road and also the efforts of those whom I have hurt. Perhaps someone cannot bring themselves to forgive me: then I must wait, while growing more deeply into repentant love. That is the main good which may emerge from an uresolved situation, but once again, it reveals how God is at work.

Rwanda 1994

'Left to Tell: Discovering God Amidst the Rwandan Holocaust' is the story of a survivor of the Rwandan genocide of 1994. The author, Immaculée Ilibagiza, gives a vivid account of the massacre itself and also of her efforts to forgive its perpetrators.

In the nineteenth century Rwanda was colonised by the Belgians who favoured the minority Tutsis over the Hutus. This created deep resentment among the Hutus, and several uprisings took place before the 1994 massacre which was orchestrated by the Hutus who were then in government. More than a million Tutsis died during the killing spree which lasted 100 days, and often those who did the killings were Hutu neighbours. Good people were brainwashed into accepting that the law of genocide was that you must kill your best friend first, else you will be killed yourself. Immaculée's Tutsi family members – father, mother and two brothers, together with seven uncles – were murdered.

Immaculée, a Catholic, survived through the kindness of a Hutu

Protestant minister. For ninety-one days she and seven other women huddled silently together in a tiny bathroom – three feet by four – in his house. Bands of machete-wielding killers hunted for her, knowing she must be hiding somewhere close by. She could hear them on the far side of the wall: 'She's here... we know she's here somewhere... Find her, find Immaculée.'

Her cramped quarters entailed high levels of physical discomfort; she and her companions had to survive on the scraps of food and water which the pastor brought. Added to all this was the fear of discovery, but what was worst for Immaculée was to have to cope with the rage and hate that flooded her heart as news slowly came in that those she loved had died brutally and that her home and village had been ravaged and burnt down. She prayed endlessly, and came to see that her own heart needed healing: she asked God to empty her of her desire to kill those who had killed her family.

Having escaped to a French military camp she finally met the man who had killed her family: her heart melted with pity for him. Now in jail, he was a broken man, full of shame and remorse, and he raised his eyes only once to hers. She reached out, touched his hands lightly, and quietly said what she had come to say: '*I forgive you*'. He was dragged back to his cell by his jailers, but the Governor, who himself had lost four children, returned to her in rage at what she had done. '*I brought that man to you to question him, to spit on him if you wished. But you forgave him. How could you do that? Why did you forgive him?*' She answered him with the truth. '*Forgiveness is all I have to offer.*'

Never Too Late to Forgive

Fifteen years after the genocide Immaculée had her home rebuilt, held a party for all sides, and then donated the house to the village as a safe place in which to pursue peace and forgiveness. A great cheer went up and Hutu and Tutsi joined together in prayer. Immaculée now devotes her life to spreading the message of peace and reconciliation across the world. She has visited Belfast and the Peace Wall, and has set up a foundation to help the orphaned children of Rwanda and elsewhere. Her witness to the healing power of God's love and forgiveness is bearing fruit in Rwanda itself. The guilty have been imprisoned and tried and those who ask forgiveness are now being restored to their old towns and villages.

People everywhere have been touched by Immaculée's witness to the process of forgiveness. A woman whose parents had been killed in the Holocaust told her how she had been full of anger her entire life, but that hearing her story now enabled her to forgive. A 92-year old lady said, 'I thought it was too late for me to forgive. I've been waiting to hear someone say what you did – I had to know that it was possible to forgive the unforgivable.'

Transformation From Inside

The story of Immaculee points to our theme: that God is at work in evil, drawing good from it. We have noted already that there are no quick-fixes on God's part. History slowly unfolds, and we cannot see how it will end. But from what we have explored thus far some gleams of light emerge which illustrate God's long-range strategies to cope with human evil.

God is at work on our *inner transformation,* and works with us individually, so the divine project is achieved only slowly rather than in dramatic numbers. God labours to bring us into the *koinonia,* that final community of love, comprising the Father, Son, Spirit and all human beings. Through this inner work, we are to become like God in our loving, else we will not be at home with the three divine Persons and with those who are already with God. There is no hatred, no negativity, no resentment in God, so our hearts must be purified of the residues that can silt up the wellspring of love in our hearts. Slowly we must learn to return love for hate, good for evil, simply because God does so. We would speed up the process of eliminating evil; we'd zap the evil-doers, as Immaculee wished she could do, when she imagined at one point that if she had a Rambo-style gun she would kill all Hutu killers. But this brings her to realise that she has murder in her heart, just as her intending killers had. Her struggle to resist hardening her heart was huge. In Ignatian terms what was going on in her was the struggle between the two spirits, one of darkness, the other of light.

The Example of Jesus

Jesus enables our conversion from the disastrous pattern of tit-for-tat retaliation to a level of forgiveness that is divine. He is the innocent victim, treated maliciously by those to whom he brought Good News. He endures the Cross, the symbol of shame. He accepts the worst that his torturers can do to him and remains loving, forgiving. The Cross shows that God is FOR us all *to the uttermost* (John 13:1). On Calvary Jesus becomes a life-giving spectacle for those who can see. He encompasses evil by his forgiving love. This is the 'love of another kind' that shines out in him.

We experience his mercy towards ourselves, and gradually learn to share it with others who offend us. Forgiving love is transformative, and slowly we become good as God is. Contemplation of Jesus' forgiving love is critical for our growth; hence Christian liturgy revolves around it, as in the Eucharist and the Easter ceremonies. C S Lewis recounts that as a schoolboy, if he wanted to get a sick-day, he snuggled up beside a boy who had the measles, and the infection did the rest. He goes on to say that if you want to be wet, you must go out into the rain or stand in a shower, and if you want to share in life-giving forgiveness, you need to stay close to the one who has it. He refers to this process as 'good infection'.

The Transformation of Evil

In the dynamic of the Cross we find a signpost that the way to fight evil is to take the road of love. Evil and suffering have a hidden positive element in them: they can be the occasion of our inner transformation. Our hearts are broken by evil and pain, but they can also be broken open to great love. Evil, strangely, can bring out the best in us. We can arrive at a place where we love as God loves, which is the whole purpose of human living.

Seeing Enemies With New eyes

'Enemy' comes from the Latin *in-imicus,* meaning 'one who is not a friend' *(amicus).* This or that person whom I cannot tolerate happens to be *'a brother or sister for whom Christ died'* (1 Corinthians 8:11)! But Jesus dies for all, so my 'enemies' must be included, whether I like it or not. This can transform my way of looking at them, and it justifies Pope Francis' statement quoted earlier: *'When everything is said and done, we are infinitely loved.'* So I can love the actual and potential goodness in them. This is God's perspective on them – and on me too, since as yet I am not fully good.

My 'enemies' challenge my heart to limitless expansion. Just as I need others to make space for me in my wrongdoing and inadequacy, so I must make space for them. Immaculee's statements, *'I forgive you'* and *'Forgiveness is all I have to offer'* are magnificent. Forgiveness, acceptance, tolerance, mercy – these are our gift to the world and they advance the process of the world's redeeming.

Living In Forgiving Mode

To live in forgiving mode each day is what is asked of me. I have been sinned against but I also wound others. I must ask and bestow forgiveness as needed. To hold off is to remain on the periphery of that final community to which the passport is 'reconciliation'. But in the depths of my heart there lurk instincts of revenge, retaliation, disgust, indifference, dismissiveness. These are not of God and I must work steadily on them.

My prayer gives a good indicator of where I stand: Jesus' commands me to '*forgive from the heart*' (Matthew 18:35). He adds, '*Whenever you stand praying, forgive, if you have anything against anyone*' (Mark 11:25). I must beg to be freed to love with forgiving love. Only then can I help to break down the barriers that delay the coming of the final community of love. Immaculee was called to forgive, and rose to the challenge. I also am called to be part of the solution rather than the problem. God doesn't like working alone!

Do I feel hurt not only when evil knocks at my door but when it knocks at the door of another? Or am I a diseased and nerveless limb that cannot feel the pain in the other members of Christ's Body? Do I intercede – not superficially but profoundly – for a tragic world?

Solidarity in Sin and Grace

So long as I deliberately exclude anyone, no matter how bad, from my love, I am imprisoned, burdened, unfree, warped, ill at ease, distanced from God. Hating takes up a great deal of energy. The tug of grace won't let me rest until I let my enemy in. God persists in 'making me grow in love' as the old translation of the second Eucharistic Prayer put it. So far as I close my heart to anyone I perpetuate a warped world.

How far am I still an Old Testament person, who simply wishes that the wicked would disappear, painfully if possible? Is the light of the New Testament getting in through my darkened and shuttered windows? Am in caught in sincere pride which prevents me from accepting that I am in solidarity with a sinful race? Living with evil-doers is hard; for example, the company of paedophiles is demanding, so the Church community tends to airbrush them out in ways that seem incompatible with the Gospels. But it is not my privilege to condemn anyone. '*Who am I to judge?*' as Pope Francis said. Mercy encompasses me and all my brothers and sisters.

Jesus chose to '*eat with sinners*' and to be crucified in the company of a thief and an insurrectionist. Would I turn down his invitation to a meal in the hope of more exclusive company? I belong to a large dysfunctional family called the human race. There is no better-established family I could join. We are part of one another, and he is at the centre of it, setting the pace and the atmosphere, revealing what forgiving love is like.

'REMEMBER THE BAD!'

The following extraordinary prayer of a Jew who died during the Holocaust turns on its head the challenge to forgive. Hatred turns to gratitude!

> *Lord, when you enter your glory, do not remember only people of good will. Remember also those of ill will. Do not remember their cruelty and violence. Instead, be mindful of the fruits we bore because of what they did to us. Remember the patience of some and the courage of others. Recall the camaraderie, humility, fidelity and greatness of soul which they awoke in us. And grant, O Lord, that the fruits we bore may one day be their redemption.*

FOR REFLECTION

Spend a little time with this prayer, because it offers a rich gleam of light on the transformation of evil. Can you see some meaning in it?

Can you find any 'persons of ill will' as this Jew did, whom you can now thank because they widened your heart? If you find one, you will find a second. Looking back on your own life ask yourself if you are growing in forgiveness: if you find you are 'stuck' ask God to soften your heart.

FINDING GOD IN WHAT IS BAD

When leading workshops on Ignatian spirituality, I begin by inviting the group to search for the presence of God in all things. They have little difficulty in recounting experiences of finding God in the good things of their lives. It is easy to find the beauty of God in creation, or the love of God in a good heart, or the helpful touch of God in situations that turn out well. God is the Great Lover *'who gives all to the beloved, and wishes to give his very self to us, so far as he can'* – St Ignatius says this, based on his personal experience, and he invites us to become people with ever-growing gratitude. It is not hard to fall in love with beauty, and as Hopkins says, *'give beauty back, beauty, beauty, beauty back to God, beauty's self and beauty's giver.'* God wants to be found, and is often only thinly disguised. God is the One *'from whom all good things* come' as the liturgy puts it: everything good is a hint of the goodness of God. For more on this, see my *Finding God in All Things*.

Finding God in the Bad

But finding God in the bad is more difficult. If *'finding God'* means making the connections between things and God, how do we do this in regard to suffering and evil?

The word *betrayed* is used of Jesus as he enters his passion, and we can use it as an umbrella term for the fact that so much lets us down. Partnerships fail; good projects get undermined; illness weakens us; people in public life deceive us. If we're honest we sometimes feel that God too betrays us. Here the task of finding God becomes more demanding. The more you become aware of the presence of God in what is good, the more you experience the gap in the scheme of things. All is not good. The best of situations is bordered by anxiety: nothing in this world lasts for ever. Where is God in what is dark?

Ignatius includes the darker realities when he asks us to find God in everything. With his shattered leg and his stomach problems he was no stranger to physical suffering, and he must have had to work hard to find God there. On a deeper level he endured the shortcomings of the Church of his time, which was then Christian only in name. Interrogated eight times by the Inquisition, he endured the possibility that his newly founded Order might be closed down. He speaks of '*the sad misery of this life*' in reference to the frustrations he endured in his dealings with people. He knew from the inside the experience of desolation – that numbing sense of hopelessness, loss of faith in God, inner darkness, temptations to give up.

Like him, we sometimes imagine that we are on our own, that God is far away, that things are against us and that our meagre resources are not fit for purpose. When things begin to grow dark and desolation sets in, we feel in tune with Yeats' line: '*Things fall apart; the centre cannot hold. Mere anarchy is loosed upon the world*'. But that is only the surface reality: at the heart of things something profound and good is going on. As Hopkins puts it: '*There lives the dearest freshness deep down things.*'

What To Do in the Dark

Ignatius' advice is that I must try to '*keep God always before my eyes.*' In desolation I should not abandon the good I can do. I can steady myself by recalling God's goodness, God's mighty deeds of which we have spoken earlier. Only on this foundation can I effectively face the difficult dimensions of life and believe that evil has its limits, whereas goodness and love do not. I try to hold on to the conviction that I am in harmony with God, despite all that may be going wrong, and that God is *labouring* with me, as Ignatius puts it. God too can find human history hard going! I can ask God, '*What ought I do?*' I find it helps in times of desolation to do someone a kindness, no matter how small. That orients me towards the light again. We find God easiest among our suffering sisters and brothers. If I sense that God wants me to get involved in some messy situation, I set about the task, but *with God*, not alone. This sense of the companionship of God gets me into positive mode, and also saves me from acting out of anger. Instead I can find a love and compassion which come from God.

By doing something positive and loving, I loosen the grip of the power of darkness on me. I have my unique role in the scheme of things. It will include the task of bringing love into fractured relationships. St Augustine's dictum, *'For evil to succeed it is enough for good persons to do nothing'* is still valid, so let me do what I can. Ignatius, when faced with challenging and bad situations, would ask God, *'What ought I do?'* His 7,000 *Letters* are prosaic accounts of his interventions in the situations of his times. God is still labouring in our world. Jesus *'went about doing good'* (Acts 10:38), and so must I as his disciple. My task is to work with God in the darkness and the mess to shape *'a kingdom of truth and life, of holiness and grace, of justice, love and peace'*. I must – patiently or impatiently – endure the divine delays in the emergence of that final resolution of all things.

Everything Converging

To find God in the bad it helps to imagine a God who is Life Itself, a God who is out in front, leading humankind forward – somewhat like the pillar of cloud and the pillar of fire that encouraged the Hebrews as they wandered in the desert. I can imagine that this God is drawing everything together – all the bits and pieces that are falling apart – and that I have a part to play here. Teilhard de Chardin asserts on the basis of *Ephesians* that the cosmic Christ draws creation to himself. If you go back to that text, you will see that the Great divine Plan is underway, gathering up all things in Christ, things in heaven and things on earth.

How do you imagine the cosmos? Is it evolving in some haphazard way of its own accord, or is it being rolled out by God like a great carpet? Is it being irresistibly drawn forward by God who is out in front? I imagine the pieces of the cosmic jigsaw being caught up and assembled in some divine space, so that not one is lost: through the divine imagination the crooked and warped pieces all find a home. We have mentioned the law of gravity whereby large bodies draw smaller bodies irresistibly to themselves: is there also a divine gravity which draws everything to itself, good but also bad, successes but also failures, grace but also sin and evil?

The random sweepings of the universe, according to the scientists, become stars and planets – and they become human beings too. We are made of the dust of the earth but we have become the images and the temples of God! God is extravagant and indiscriminate in loving. The bad as well as the good are welcomed, and we must not set limits to divine lavishness, else there will be no hope for any of us. What now seems fit only to be discarded can be integrated into the final glory of things. I too am in that energy field, that cosmic dynamic, because physical and spiritual energy is always flowing out from God, the Omega point, to me.

This energy empowers, illuminates and loves me. I can appropriate it, depend on it and then play my part in the unfolding of the world as God indicates. The contemplative reflection mentioned earlier flows from such a vision: I can tap into and contribute to that spiritual vitality that *'reaches from end to end of the universe'*. Suffering and evil can indeed threaten to overwhelm me; but *they do not overwhelm God*, who is working to bring good out of them. Somehow, sometime, they will be resolved. From that awareness I can change, as Ignatius puts it, from being weak and sad to being strong and joyous.

I LEAVE MY LITTLENESS BEHIND!

Jane Fonda's recent book, Prime Time, *is full of encouragement for those who are in their later years. But her final chapter, 'Full Tilt to the End' tells of a fourteen-year-old who was distressed by her parents' recent divorce. To escape her misery she used walk her dog in New York's Central Park. There she meets with a Frenchman called Mr Tayer. He is imaginative, playful and funny. They become friends and he asks her what will she become. He invites her not to live only out of a small portion of herself, because human beings are pilgrims of the future, they are being drawn into the dimensions of the spirit, and that spirit fulfils itself in a personal God. She chats with her mother about her meetings, and tells her that when she meets with Mr Tayer she leaves her littleness behind. His final words to her are, 'Remain always true to yourself, but move ever upward toward greater consciousness and greater love'. Only years later does she discover that her 'Mr Tayer' was none other than Teilhard de Chardin.*

Teilhard, a Jesuit priest, had a unique vision of the presence of God in creation. However he suffered greatly at the hands of the Church, and the Jesuit Order found him too much to handle. His evolutionary ideas were seen as threatening to Catholic faith in France, so he was exiled to China where he worked for twenty years. When the Communists took over he returned to France, but was still unwelcome there and moved to New York. His greatest works, including The Divine Milieu *and* The Phenomenon of Man, *although written in the 1920s and '30s, were not allowed to be published until after his death in 1955.*

Only posthumously did he gain the stature his thinking deserved, and his breadth of vision had a profound influence on Vatican II. He bore all his betrayals patiently and as the incident related by Jane Fonda indicates, he did not lapse into cynicism or depression, but kept alive his vision that God is indeed working in everything. For him the Incarnation is a making new, a restoration, of all the universe's forces and powers. Despite all appearances, the world is a holy place, full of sacred associations; we are steeped in the divine and nothing is profane. With Christ at the centre we are to harness for God the energies of love around us, and thus transform our world.

FOR REFLECTION

Have you ever come across someone who gave you hope and vision when life was difficult? What do you think kept Teilhard going in his long years of exile and frustration? Can you turn your experiences of depression and rejection into positive energy as he did?

THE 'AMEN' OF MY LIFE

'Last scene of all,
that ends this strange eventful history,
is second childishness and mere oblivion'.

So Shakespeare writes in *As You Like It*. Does life end in oblivion? Is life 'but a walking shadow, 'full of sound and fury, signifying nothing'? Or is there more to us than that?

The following simple exercise can help you to integrate the light and the dark, the joys and the sorrows of your life. It offers a lens through which you can gaze contemplatively on how things have been. We have described contemplation as 'taking a long, loving look at the real' – not just at the real in its beauty but in its disfigurement too. This is how God sees you. All can be gathered up and find its eternal place!

I invite you to take a blank sheet. On the top left write, *'Dear God'* and at the bottom right put your name, and underneath it *'Amen'*. Let the space in the middle be filled – in imagination at least – with the history of your life, its activities and accomplishments, its endurings, its sufferings, its failures and its dyings. Hand all these over to God, and ask God to bring good out of them.

The final word, *Amen*, is richer than we think. *Amen* can be a stamp of firm commitment. Here it says, *'Lord, this is the song of my life. It's flat in places and I have bungled the words here and there, but it's me. I love you and dedicate my song to you.'* In the legend of St Jerome's meeting with Jesus in the desert, Jesus asks him what he has to give him. Jerome lists his labours, his penances, his prayers. Silence ensues, then Jesus says, *'Give me also your sins!'* Absolutely everything can be included on my blank page!

Our days and years are like the water-pots at Cana: they need the creating word of God to be turned into *'the best wine at the last'*. God can and will do this for our water-pots. So *Amen* can mean, *'Dear God, I hereby commit my life to you, in all its shades, bright and dark. I trust that in your goodness and compassion you will transform it all into something worthwhile.'*

By doing this exercise now you can make your final option for God here and now rather than delay it till you are incapable of making choices.

You can also do this exercise on behalf of people you love who could not do it for themselves, or who died suddenly and unexpectedly. One of my colleagues collapsed and died recently at age forty-six. He was at the height of his career, and from what I knew of him, death was far from his mind. Since he has come into my mind today I will take a little time to hold a private service for him on the lines I have sketched above, offering him and every detail of his life to God.

To Be As Christ Is

The 'Amen' of our lives can be drawn out for a long time. I mentioned in the Acknowledgements my sick brethren in the Jesuit Nursing Home in Dublin whom I join for the celebration of the Sunday Eucharist. I said that their patient acceptance of their varying situations is an ongoing lesson for me. They are a motley crew, gathered together by the ravages of ageing, strokes, dementia and accidents. One, when lecturing in Rome, was hit by a motorbike and has been unable to speak since; another was working in Zambia and was left brain-damaged after a violent assault; a third has endured progressive blindness and Parkinson's. Meals are frequently silent: some can no longer speak, others can no longer hear.

In terms of Jesus' parable of the Sower, their lives are 'good soil' because it is being harrowed over and over again. Harrowing breaks down the soil and unlocks its potential. The seed planted in such soil dies indeed but only to bear much fruit when harvest time comes around. The rhythms of the universe play out: we began as cosmic dust: we became stardust walking tall, and then we crumble away to the dust from which we came. These men on their Zimmers and in their wheelchairs carry their mystery of passivity silently. Their task is 'to pray for the Church and the Society' but what we think of as the capacity to pray is disappearing with all else. Their hollowing out is nearly complete. Their one-time hopes, ambitions, preferences are all being smoothed away. Their 'Amen' is said. They await what Hopkins hints at in his poem, *That Nature is a Heraclitean Fire and of the comfort of the Resurrection:*

> *In a flash, at a trumpet crash,*
> *I am all at once what Christ is, | since he was what I am, and*
> *This Jack, joke, poor potsherd, | patch, matchwood, immortal diamond,*
> *Is immortal diamond.*

Now diamonds can be anything up to four billion years old. They are formed from volcanic rock which erupts from deep within the earth's crust, under intense pressure and heat. As for my friends, they have been what Christ was in his passion; their mode of transfiguration into immortal diamonds is less dramatic but no less sure and mysterious. I greet them the days I meet them, and bless when I understand.

ALL I ASK OF YOU

I was by my mother's bedside. She had had a stroke, and I who for years had tried to keep her going, could do nothing. I felt more helpless than ever before in my life. I was wrestling with God about justice and mercy, and how unfair life is. I wasn't getting too far!

But then I had this quiet sense that God was saying to me, 'That's my problem, not yours!' And I felt such peace and reassurance that a huge weight was lifted from my shoulders. For a time afterward I felt as if I were floating on a cloud: such a sense of peace, of being heard and understood.

It wasn't that God was saying to me, 'Mind your own business!' It was more like a promise: 'You can trust me on this!' I was being quietly invited just to sit there and do nothing but attend. And I did, and doing nothing was ok. I felt as if the job I'd burdened myself with – of making sense of things, of saving someone from their pain – had been taken away from me. And shortly before she died my Mother said, 'All I ask of you is that you remember me as loving you! Nothing else matters.' The line was from an old hymn, and she had stored it till the end, as a gift to me.

I still wonder about unfairness and injustice, but mostly I can now leave them be, together with the other frustrations I experience. They are part of the 'Amen' of my life.

FOR REFLECTION

If you do the 'Amen' exercise I have suggested, you will surely find that there are passages of your life of which you are not too proud. Do you wonder, 'Am I good enough for God?'

But human imperfection is not a problem to God: creation itself is not 'perfect' yet God asserts that it is 'good'. So can you say to God as my mother said to me, 'Remember me as loving you'? Surely that will be 'good enough' for God!

IS DYING ALL BAD? A REFLECTION

Some years ago I wrote a book called *To Grow in Love: The Spirituality of Ageing*. Kindly readers said they liked it, but they regretted that it said very little about death! My apology was that 'I don't know enough about it – yet!' Death is the most mysterious reality of all: those who speak don't know, and those who know don't speak. I find the silence of the dead awesome and unnerving, and all the more so as my time runs out!

For many people death can appear as the worst of evils, so the following reflection may be helpful.

> *'Lord, most of us think of death as bad. I grieve over the deaths of those I love and I struggle against my own mortality. Yet I also meet people who are patiently waiting for God to take them home. So Lord, is death all bad?*
>
> *As a child I trusted the promises my parents made, and usually things worked out, despite anxious waiting on my part. When my mother was sorting out my little disasters, she would say, 'Don't worry, I'll make it better.' If she went away she promised she'd be back soon, and she did return. Promises are the language of love. Lord, since you too are good and faithful you promise to return to take me with you so that I can be where you are – in a glory and joy that will not end. These great promises invite me to trust that death is only an in-between moment in which we pass from darkness into light and joy.*
>
> *Nevertheless, Lord, it would help a lot if people came back from the dead to reassure us that all is well with them. Even a word, a whisper, would help enormously, but there is this unearthly silence. No doubt you have your reasons for withholding this gift. You ask me to live in trust and hope. And how easily it has slipped*

my memory that one of us, who was also your Son, died as we do, rose from the dead into a new dimension of life and did return to bring us the good news that at death we are welcomed into the fullness of life.

Lord, keep that great promise in my mind when I imagine that dying is the end rather than the Great Beginning! I get things the wrong way round: forgive my feebleness. Let me think of this life as a prelude to the Great Symphony, a preparation for the Big Game, an introduction to my endless Love Affair with you.

For you, it's relationships that endure, and you have gone to a lot of trouble to win my friendship. Don't let me wait until the end to realise that your friendship is to be the heart of my life even now. So often I avoid you. My prayer record is not too impressive: over the long years how much quality time have I set aside for us to meet? In death, thankfully, you will re-establish the right order of things; you will be everything to me, and that will be good. Death won't be all that bad if this happens. Will I break down then in belated thanks for your kindness? Let me thank you now and fill my remaining days with gratitude.

Coming Home

You promise not just that I will be happy after death the way children are happy in a playground even while their parents are at a distance, but rather that I will meet you face to face. You made me so that we could be together forever. I need you, I am need for you. Else I'm nothing, gone like a puff of smoke. But with you I will become fully alive, I'll be at my best, glorious and immortal. Death is your way of calling me home. Sometime, not too far off, you will whisper to me, 'May I walk you home?' As always you are the One who takes the good initiatives in my life. True, when I am dying I will have to say goodbye to all those I love, but it's really an 'au revoir' – 'until we see each other again'! And you *will be there awaiting me, or better, you will run to meet me like the Prodigal Father. You will put the best robe on me, the ring, the sandals. You will kiss me. And with you will be all those whom I loved in this life – family, friends, beloveds, and even those I found hard to cope with. But they, like me, will also be at their best, and this will ease things!*

I am a visitor on this earth, a pilgrim, but I often forget this. The Hebrews had a better sense of home as being where you are. They lamented times of exile, whether in Egypt, or in the desert, or in Babylon. They longed to get back home, to rest, to be close to you. Increase that longing in me! When we meet, you will gaze on me and smile as you have always done, and you'll look for a glad smile from me in return. As a parent gazes at a child's face, hoping for a smile of recognition, you will recognise me as your own. Will you call me by my name as you called Mary of Magdala after you rose? And will I do as she did and call you 'Master' or will I perhaps dare to whisper 'Abba'? Will I be shy, dumbfounded, 'gob-smacked' as we say? Will I manage even a smile? It would be good if I learnt to smile more at you even now. Will you set me at ease by inviting me to 'come and have breakfast', as you invited Peter and his companions at the lakeside? Will you open my eyes to see that you were present in all my hopes, disappointments, achievements and failures? Only then will I understand that indeed you worked in all things for my good. And will you invite me to bring to you my little catch of fish? For you tell us that 'our good deeds go with us' and that no action done in love will lose its reward. When you ask me the only question that matters to you, 'Brian, do you love me?' I hope Peter will be there to prompt me to say, 'Lord, you know everything; you know I love you'. Perhaps I will only be able to nod, but that will be enough: you read my heart unerringly always.

Transfiguration

> *In death, Lord, you will overwhelm me. Please go gently, because I am earthbound and unused to dramatic visits from the divine. You will transfigure me, body, heart and soul, as you yourself were transfigured on the mountain. This will be a 'makeover' like none other, and it may make me laugh with glad surprise! You will search my love, and bring out the best in me. When you start to thank me for having been 'good and faithful', surely I will begin to cry. Are those tears something of what they mean by Purgatory? But with your help I will not get lost in remorse – that would be self-centred. Instead I will become authentic, good, radiant. Does all this occur in an instant, as in a moment of psychotherapy when I suddenly see the truth and am set free? The prodigal son had that experience: he wasn't dragged through the mud but instead accepted for what he was, he was loved through and through. How did he feel when he was the guest of honour? Will this be me? Will I be shy and demure then, with all the starch washed out of me? Will I be truly humble for the first time? That would be good, Lord! But don't let me be awkward: let me give in and share your joy to the full. Perhaps I can even increase your joy: the Gospels mention that there will be 'more joy in heaven' at the arrival of the likes of me than of the saints. You are mysterious in the company you prefer!*

Eternally Grateful

> *I have been known to complain against you when things broke my heart or the hearts of those I love. But I will have no complaints then: the suffering and the waiting will be forgotten; I will see how you wove them into my life: how they became the making of me. When I catch on to what you were trying to do, I shall be silently grateful and overcome. Often I have thought of you as distant, remote: but in death I will see your caring hand and your saving interventions in every detail. All the known and unknown disasters*

141

I've been saved from! Often I've missed the point and sailed on regardless, not realising you were watching out for me. In this life I catch on only fitfully to the fact that you are the perfect friend, always wishing me well, standing by me in my failings, setting up moments of growth for me every day of my life. But when we meet I will be startled into full awareness. Then I will say a 'Thank you' such as I have never said before. It might do me no harm to practise that 'Thank you' even now, today...

Not only will I blossom and become radiant, but our friendship will come to its perfection, and with it, my friendship with all your friends and mine who will crowd around, congratulating me. The experience of being totally loved and forgiven will impel me to ask and offer forgiveness everywhere it's needed. There will be unending joy in this for all of us.

Truly, Lord, if death is the entry point into such joy, then it is not all bad.

PART FIVE
THE UNFINISHED EPIC OF PLANET EARTH

WILL ALL BE SAVED?

A Question of Justice

We have a passion for fairness: wrong-doing, we believe, must be punished. But is this how God thinks? Is God 'fair' in dealing with evil-doers? We have mentioned earlier the issue of the salvation of all humankind: it is the final moment of God's response to the problem of evil, and we need to explore it more fully.

Pope Benedict XVI, in his encyclical on Hope, 2008, states his conviction that the resolution of the question of injustice constitutes the strongest argument in favour of belief in eternal life. The injustice of history should not be the final word. Justice and mercy must both be satisfied, and this can be done only beyond the reach of evil-doing, in other words, in a dimension beyond our own. There, evil will be finally dealt with. If there is to be an all-inclusive community of love at the End, all the factors that impede it must be sorted out.

In the Pope's view, redeeming grace cannot be like a sponge which simply wipes evil away as if nothing really mattered. Evildoers cannot sit at table at the eternal banquet beside their victims as though there were no bad history to be resolved. Repentance and forgiveness will be key dynamics binding the community together. Before the gaze of God all falsehood will melt away. The encounter with God after death will reveal the truth of our lives. God's gaze will heal us of our wrong-doing through a painful transformation. His love will sear through us like a flame, enabling us to become totally ourselves and thus totally of God. This transforming moment occurs, not in chronological time but in the heart's time: whether or not it will come to all we cannot say. But, as the Pope says, we must hope and pray that it will come to ourselves and all our sisters and brothers.

Not Without My Brother

Some years ago a Dublin family decided to bring a child home from the local orphanage for Christmas day. When the father arrived at the orphanage a little girl was sitting waiting for him. 'Are you all set?' he asked. 'No' she said fiercely, 'I won't come without my little brother!' 'Of course!' he said. The pair had a great day, and the family loved them so much that they adopted both, and they are now living happy lives.

The little girl in our tale mirrors the attitude of Jesus in our regard. She would forego her own happiness for the sake of her brother. Jesus does likewise. He would not willingly come home to his Father without us – *all of us!* God's intention is to do whatever is needed to bring all of us into eternal joy. While this seems impossible to us, given the depth of human malice, nothing is impossible to God. Each of us '*is a brother or sister for whom Christ died*' (Romans 14:15). Jesus states at the Last Supper, *'I will come and take you to myself, so that where I am you may be also'* (Jn 14:3).

Some theologians simply assert – on the basis of the goodness and mercy of God – that everyone will be saved. But the Church expresses sober *hope*, not certainty, on the issue. She has never declared anyone to be in hell, not even Judas. We are to *pray* for the salvation of all as in the trimming to the Rosary: *'Lead all souls to heaven, especially those most in need of your mercy.'*

Liturgy expresses the same boundless hope. The first Eucharistic Prayer for Reconciliation calmly states, *'You have bound the human family to yourself… with a new bond of love so tight that it can never be undone.'* If we draw out the implications of that statement it carries us far along the way.

Gentler Teaching

But how can the Church reconcile this hope for the salvation of everyone with its own tradition that those who die in mortal sin go to hell?

There has been a significant softening in Church teaching about eternal damnation over the past twenty years. The *Catholic Catechism* of 1992 teaches the following:

> *The affirmations of Sacred Scripture and the teachings of the Church on the subject of hell are a call to the responsibility incumbent on us to make use of our freedom in view of our eternal destiny. They are at the same time an urgent call to conversion* (1036).

Again:

> *The message of the Last Judgment calls people to conversion while God is still giving them 'the acceptable time... the day of salvation'. It inspires a holy fear of God and commits them to the justice of the Kingdom of God* (1041).

These statements mean that references to eternal loss are to be interpreted as dramatic wake-up calls, no more, no less.

But surely it remains true that many die in mortal sin and therefore are in hell?

Again the Catholic Catechism cautions us to abstain from judgment:

> *Mortal sin is a radical possibility of human freedom, as is love itself... Our freedom has the power to make choices for ever, with no turning back. However, although we can judge that an act is in itself a grave offence, we must entrust judgement of persons to the justice and mercy of God* (1861). ... *We should not despair of the salvation of those who have taken their own lives... The Church prays for (such) persons'* (2283).

New Testament texts speaking of hell and damnation are to be interpreted more gently than before. They are not previews or advance notices of a disastrous end for sinners, but challenges for us to meet the needs of our neighbour in whom God dwells.

Surely Not So-and-so?

The doors of heaven are wide open to sinners, so that includes us all; and of course to non-believers, whose salvation we used to worry so much about when we believed that outside the visible Church there is no salvation. All of us, Christian or other, will be examined on our love, rather than on our beliefs. We have spoken earlier about those who have been sources of great evil and suffering to others. Perhaps the flaws in their psychological make-up will excuse them; perhaps the Jew's prayer for his persecutors will prevail, because it will be seen that their wrong-doing has brought great goodness to birth in others. Perhaps God is not very selective and takes a global view, as happened when he promised to spare Sodom and Gomorrah if ten righteous people could be found in it (Genesis 18:32). Again, God shepherded the whole horde of the Hebrew slaves, good and bad, across the Red Sea. God doesn't seem to examine our credentials too closely! Human solidarity may be enough to ensure that no-one gets left out at the End. God, after all, is indiscriminate and extravagant in loving. That is what it means to be divine.

Hope for the salvation of all was strongly held in earlier Christian tradition. Long obscured by pessimism, it has now re-emerged as an open possibility. Since the middle ages a steady line of female witnesses have kept alive Christian hope for the salvation of all. Their thought is encapsulated in Julian of Norwich's 'All will be well!' The French Catholic writer Paul Claudel (d. 1955) echoes the early belief in his delightful faith-filled comment: *'Sinners, deprived of daylight, worship in the night!'* Teilhard de Chardin says to God: *'You have told me O God, to believe in hell. But you have forbidden me to hold with absolute certainty that any human being has been damned'*. We can reasonably hope that hell may be empty.

146

God Risks Everything

What stands behind the Christian hope that no-one may be lost? It is the Cross, which proclaims from the hilltop of Calvary that we are loved, forgiven, wanted, awaited, never rejected; the hand of divine friendship is never withdrawn. All we need is to accept it. While certainty about universal salvation is not stated, Christ's victory over sin and death can be understood in its widest dimensions. Because God is so totally invested in our salvation, the scales tilt hugely in our favour. There is the story of the Rabbi who confesses to God that he has despaired of his wayward flock. To which God thunders in reply: 'Go back to my people! I have sunk myself in them!'

Nothing is impossible to God who has gone so far as to make even hell a Christological place by Jesus' visit there after his death. Is there a person, human or angelic, who can remain closed to that love which can *'subdue the whole universe'* (Philippians 3:21)?

A WAITING GOD

An old story describes Peter at the gates of heaven. The world has ended. The faithful are inside and Peter is preparing to close the gates. Then he sees Jesus standing outside. 'Master' he says, 'what are you doing outside?' Jesus replies, 'I'm waiting for Judas.'

REFLECTION

When I find myself in a queue, am I anxious for the people behind me, or only for myself? Do I care about the salvation of all the rest, if only I can get inside the pearly gates myself?

A child asked: 'What gets God out of bed in the morning?' Surely we can say it is an endless care for all humankind. Do I share this care?

THE GREAT EPIC

A theologian friend of mine used to speak of human history in terms of an extended joke. A joke puzzles and disconcerts us until the final word is spoken and the meaning becomes clear. Then tension is released in laughter. Try the following simple story as an example of how a joke works: A friend of mine, a Sister, was living in a poor area. She was on her way home on a dark winter evening when she caught up with a woman who was dragging a long metal pole. Her offer to help was accepted, and as they trudged along, one at either end of the pole, she said, *'May I ask what this is for?' 'It's for making a clothes-line'* was the answer from the far end. *'And what is it?'* asked the curious Sister. From the far end came the reply, *'A bus stop'*.

God must indeed love a good story, given the complexity of human history! At the End we will tell our stories, and as we unearth the hidden meaning in them, we will laugh merrily together with God, for God has an immense sense of humour. As of now, we see only the outlines of the Great Epic. God's great saving deeds are in place – Creation, Exodus, Redemption, and God's ongoing work in human history. But how my personal story fits in I do not yet see. The punch-line has not yet come. The comment of the lion Aslan at the close of CS Lewis' *Narnia Tales* teaches me to be patient: *'I tell no one any story but their own'*.

Agony and Ecstasy

But the promise is given that we shall laugh (Luke 6:21). Victory is assured. God will wipe away all tears. There will be no more death and mourning (Revelation 21:4). Our present suffering is not worth comparing to the glory that will be revealed in us at the End: the present is only a foil to the magnificence of the future (Romans 8:18).

Now we are like women in labour (John 16:21), but then will come the joy. Now we stumble along with limited glimpses of the complete picture. Even to get these glimpses is hard work: as we have seen, we have to grapple with the data to reveal the hidden clues, because evil is unreasonable – it cannot be understood directly.

While we must try to find God in the mess of human living, the evil itself will not reveal God's presence directly. But we can loiter with intent, searching in the evil for what Shakespeare terms the 'soul of goodness' that is hidden in it. Reflection is needed. A contemplative stance helps. Like God we must be willing to take 'a long, loving look at the real' – the real which includes both bad and good. So as we contemplate the death of Jesus we see that it is not good in itself, yet great good emerges from it – the overcoming of death for all. And so we can trust that death is not the end but an in-between moment of darkness leading to eternal light. Suffering can make us look beyond ourselves to God; so we become a bit less self-focussed. St Paul states that we have become the goodness of God (2 Corinthians 5:21). We rightly hope that this goodness will carry the day for the whole human race!

God, you are indeed breaking our hearts! But continue, because our hearts need to grow. As John Donne says so well: *'Batter my heart, three-personed God…'* Or as the Church prays: *'Make us grow in love…'* An older prayer with stark realism included the phrase *'even if with many a blow'!* We ask God to keep at us all until we're *finished,* not in the sense of being wiped out or cast aside, but in the sense of being brought to perfection, like a great work of art to which the final brush or chisel stroke is being given. Earlier we listed some dimensions of the great mystery of God's work in the world. By now, I hope, you can live with them more comfortably, and perhaps agree with St Thomas Aquinas' summary: *God is so almighty and good that he would allow no evil in all his works unless he were able to bring good out of it.*

Evil is like the unpromising material in a potential building site.

The engineers have to clear off the rubble before construction begins. But God goes differently about building what the New Testament calls the *'new Jerusalem'*, and incorporates into his design all the rubbish and garbage lying around. I was on holiday in Lanzarote recently: the little island had been covered in volcanic rock in the past few hundred years. It seemed an impossible landscape to draw beauty from, but the island had an architect, Cesar Manrique, who designed an internationally acclaimed building by working from the *inside* of the lava bubbles. He shows in stone how one can dialogue with an unpromising environment, and draw from it great beauty.

That's what God does, and we have to do likewise. We can spend our time cursing the darkness, lamenting the failures and corruption that infest all forms of public life including the Church. Or we can light a candle instead, and learn to share in the divine imagination which is endlessly engaged in drawing good from suffering and evil. The glimpses of God's working in human lives given in this book show in flesh and blood how suffering and evil can open our hearts to compassion, forgiveness, mercy and the quiet acceptance of reality as it comes to us.

All Will Be Well

At the End, as the hermit Julian of Norwich affirmed in the 14th century, all will be well. She says:

> *Deeds are done which appear so evil to us, and people suffer such terrible evils that it does not seem as though any good will ever come of them; and we sorrow and grieve over this. Our reasoning powers are so blind now that we cannot know the high, marvellous wisdom, the might and the goodness of the Holy Trinity. And this is what God means where he says, 'You shall see for yourself that all manner of things shall be well.*
>
> *And I saw that truly nothing happens by accident or luck, but*

everything by God's wise providence... We say that this is accident
or luck, but to our Lord God it is not so.

All will laugh together at the End. What will we then say about
divine Providence? Surely that God orchestrates all, and has done all
things well. Our image of God will be adequate then. We will see that
God is no Santa, yet good beyond imagining. We will see clearly then
what now we struggle to believe, that nothing is impossible to God.
God's work to remedy the damage done by evil will be seen to prevail.
Grace, that seemed so weak and inadequate for its enormous task,
will be seen to have won out. Our joy will be unbounded. We rightly
pray for the salvation of all, because this is God's desire, and God gets
what God wants! The whole cosmos will be radiant with God's glory,
and all will be well.

The Great Field Hospital

We started with the image of the jig-saw to describe the chaotic nature
of a world infected by suffering and evil. Let us end with Pope Francis'
image of the world as a vast field hospital, with God in charge.

When you watch a video of heart surgery, you see how the problem is accurately diagnosed and radical action is decided on; the needed resources are to hand for all emergencies, and the back-up staff is
ready. Theatre continues until the needed work is completed. There
emerges a hopeful prognosis. Recall the injuries noted earlier which
Clodagh Cogley sustained, and how they would have been dealt with.

The Gospels show Jesus up and about before dawn – as good sur-
geons often are – bringing healing to a sick and troubled world. But
with Jesus no longer walking this earth and curing people as he goes,
God can seem remote from human pain. We don't easily see how
God's plan is moving forward through history. But we don't have to.
To drive my Yaris I don't have to understand what goes on beneath
the bonnet; to put the light on in my office I don't have to understand

151

electricity; and because engineers know their job, my central heating will work, even though I know nothing of thermo-dynamics. In the life of Jesus, God explains enough of the divine project for me to reasonably believe that evil has been taken firmly in hand, and that healing is underway. When overwhelmed by evil we can feel that the world is in a hopeless and terminal state. But my thesis is that while we are indeed sick, we are in fact in God's recovery ward. Although we are convalescents rather than fully well, we are on call as nursing aides! We are God's workforce, wounded but also healers, as Henri Nouwen puts it. God reverences each person and every last detail of the human story, chaotic, warped and unworkable though it may seem to us, and tries to energise us to be escorts of grace to one another. The wounded can help one another. This work will draw out from us a deep and pure love as we tend gently the wounds of those who suffer. Among that multitude surely evildoers have the deepest wounds and need the most sustained and gentle care.

FINAL REFLECTION

We have been privileged to peep into the lives of Matryona, Arrupe's slum-dwellers, Viktor Frankl, Malala, Etty, Egger, Jennie, Clodagh, Immaculee, the Trappists in Algeria, and many others. Behind them all stands Jesus. Bring them before you now and thank them for their varied witness. Resolve to keep them as life-companions from whom you can draw inspiration as you make your way along. You are then in good company rather than alone as you labour to bring good out of sorrow and evil. They will intercede on your behalf and give you hope that divine wisdom can effectively integrate the dark pages of life into a magnificent and totally satisfying epic.

May it be so. AMEN!